"Those that run football have little, if any, idea of what it means to those millions that love and live football. This book illustrates how the game can be returned to those that truely understand what football is before it is lost forever: and by that I mean the fans."

Eddy Brimson

"If digested properly, this book could change football. As someone who believes football has a value that cannot and must not be measured, this book has a value that is immeasurable."

Omid Djalili

"A really important and timely book about a game that's losing its soul; a fascinating, forensic look at the ills of English football and how to cure them."

Henry Winter

Football:
The People's Shame

Football:
The People's Shame

How to Revolutionise a National Sport

Micky P. Kerr

Published by Repeater Books

An imprint of Watkins Media Ltd

Unit 11 Shepperton House

89-93 Shepperton Road

London

N1 3DF

United Kingdom

www.repeaterbooks.com

A Repeater Books paperback original 2024

1

Distributed in the United States by Random House, Inc., New York.

ISBN: 9781915672551

Ebook ISBN: 9781915672568

Printed and bound by CPI Group (UK) Ltd, Croydon, CR0 4YY

A man with new ideas is a madman, until his ideas triumph.

Marcelo Bielsa

Contents

Introduction
Thinking Systematically

The ultimate, hidden truth of the world is that it is something that we make, and could just as easily make differently.
David Graeber, *The Utopia of Rules*

This book is aimed at reforming English football's entire system of governance. In recent decades, supporters have been gradually dispossessed in what can only be described as an intergenerational defeat. *Football: The People's Shame* will explain how this process occurred and what could be done to reverse it.

There are alarm bells ringing everywhere, but the 2021 "fan-led" government review into the governance of football, *The Crouch Report*, suggested only minor reforms, leaving the wider system unchallenged. At present, a serious debate about transforming the entire governance of English football is not even on the table. I am hoping that upon completion of this book, you will be of the firm belief that it should be.

The argument made in later chapters is designed to reach out across the divide and provide common ground for all football fans, wherever they may position themselves on the wider political spectrum. Whether you consider yourself to be left-wing, right-wing or centrist is irrelevant in this context, because every football fan finds themselves subject to the same conditions — we all suffer the same lived experience. The misgovernance of football has resulted in authoritarianism, over-commercialisation and the foreign ownership of England's biggest clubs. Which political ideology could proudly lay claim to these circumstances? There is a simple truth which must be addressed: the outcomes produced by football's current model of governance suit only a hyper-wealthy elite.

Economic systems are not part of the natural world. It's impossible to stop the wind blowing or the sun shining, but it's certainly possible to create new models of governance and different economic structures. To feel trapped and exploited by an economic system is one thing, but to question its legitimacy and suggest alternatives is another step entirely. Ironically, those that do so are often labelled naïve. But when an economic system consistently produces terrible outcomes, should we not be putting it under the microscope? Should we not be at least considering new ideas?

The political conditions which facilitate the governance of any sport are always subject to change. Despite its cultural importance, the football industry is very small from an economic standpoint, thus making it susceptible to potential state intervention and political transformation. Simply put, this book will consider the possibility of democratising football through new forms of public ownership, thus creating a better framework through which to fund and govern our national game. Such measures could be achieved through democratic means — the will of the people.

Britain's recent exit from the European Union can only be viewed as beneficial to this proposed mandate because it has stripped away an entire framework of legal terms and conditions. For example, the EU Liberalisation Laws — which advocate for "free market" economic principles — could have proven to be problematic with regards to implementing any kind of state interference into the football industry. From within the EU's macro political structure, dispossessed claimants would certainly have more legal avenues through which to appeal. Whether you agree or disagree with Brexit is beside the point. For those who believe that Brexit *was* about replacing unelected rule with democratic procedure, a greater sense of autonomy and improved economic growth, then a movement to democratise English football, grant ownership rights to genuine supporters and create thousands of new jobs throughout England is certainly worth considering.

To do this, we're compelled to ask some big questions. What is the true meaning of the beautiful game? Why do people feel such an emotional, almost spiritual connection to it? And most importantly: how can football's system of governance support (as opposed to undermine) the deep emotional connections that people make with it? But before any proposals are made in any detail, we must first examine the current state of affairs, broaden our perspective and take a look at fandom's place in the bigger picture, revealing the power dynamics at play in modern football.

English Fandom

Throughout this book, appeals will be made directly to "English fandom". In this context, "English fandom" is a very broad church — it refers to every fan who supports a club competing in the English footballing pyramid, from the giants of the Premier League to the minnows of the 12th tier (or lower). From the die-hards who live and breathe for their club, to those with just a casual take-it or leave-it approach — all are incorporated under the umbrella of "English fandom".

When the pronouns of *we*, *us*, and *our*, are used throughout the text, they refer to this rather large body of people.

However, millions of people worldwide who pay TV subscriptions to watch English football could quite easily claim to meet the above criteria. So, to simplify the matter, the term "English fandom" only includes people with British citizenship or proof of British residency. With great respect, our focus will remain purely on men's English football; the Scottish, Welsh and Northern Irish footballing pyramids shall not be discussed, nor shall the women's game. Once again, this is only done for the purpose of simplicity. The author recognises that football is a sport for everyone, and the footballing culture of our home nations is cut from the same cloth.

If you're part of what has been defined as "English fandom", then this book speaks directly to you, it recognises your importance and places you on a pedestal. After all, the power to transform English football rests in your hands. The pages of this book seek to inspire and uplift English fandom, and to remind each and every one of you that football is for us — we're an extremely important aspect of it, we just need to recognise that.

The decision to lump together all swathes of English fandom into a single group also has political motivations. Understanding "*us*" as one living organism highlights our common ground and shared values, thus bringing every fan of every club closer together and recognising English fandom's potential as a potent political force, should we ever choose to become one.

Our opposition is English football's ruling elite, a far smaller group which includes the governing bodies of the FA, the Premier League, the EFL, and in a wider context, their equivalents at FIFA and UEFA. Obviously, most club owners (or groups of shareholders) belong to this group, as they have direct control over our football clubs, and therefore us as fans. A club's corporate sponsors also fall into this bracket because they have direct influence over the clubs they help to fund.

The following text is divided into three main sections. The first discusses our dispossession, whilst the second suggests how we could possibly take control for ourselves. The third section asks questions of who we are and looks at some possible strategies for creating change. This book is not attempting to offer a finalised blueprint for reform, rather its intention is to challenge existing ideas and alter mindsets. Today, many supporters find themselves on the back foot, disillusioned with the modern game's moral landscape and resigned to their fate as powerless serfs. *Football: The People's Shame* provides a more optimistic viewpoint — suggesting that something *can* be done to affect change. English fandom is passionate but equally depoliticised in its approach to football, a lion yet to awaken.

Part 1

Losing Control

The People's Game

I can assure you, it's much, much more important than that.
Bill Shankly

If you know, you know. Football is not just a game; it's a quasi-religious faith. We pray, obsess, fall to pieces, scream, cry, hold our breath, grit our teeth and clench our fists. Yet when we rejoice, we do so in a manner that only believers can understand. Connected, we live in the moment. All are equal inside here; there is no hierarchy. The outside world does not matter, it has no bearing or influence because, for the duration of a match, we're allowed to lose control and break free from usual societal expectations.

Sometimes we experience something that no words could ever truly describe. Moments of ecstasy are always fleeting, but they exist, and they can only exist because we have prayed, obsessed, fallen apart, screamed, cried, held our breath, gritted our teeth and clenched our fists. Without the agonising tension, there can be no release. In a world that has become so sanitised and numbing, we have found something that makes us feel.

Football has layers. The concepts of community and togetherness are central, but it can also be felt at the individual level as something spiritual and personal. Millions are hooked on the beautiful game, but each and every person's pathway to realising their affinity with football is unique. When you're a child, certain magical moments define your relationship with the game: that incredible player, that amazing goal, that special day. There is also the influence of your family and friends in enhancing your connection. Football is just what we do here, part of our DNA, culture and daily life. Its rules and rituals are deeply embedded from an early age.

My childhood belonged to football — if I wasn't watching it, I was playing it. I can still remember practising kick-ups with my best friend on the school grass during the late 1980s; my record was four (I celebrated wildly). Aged nine, I watched the 1990 World Cup unfold alongside my father on a tiny TV in our kitchen. I'll never forget that semi-final penalty defeat because it's the first time I realised that life isn't a perfect fairytale. It wouldn't surprise me if I remembered the 1990 World Cup on my deathbed — my last thoughts would be of Bobby Robson, Gary Lineker, Gazza, my father and that tiny kitchen TV. Despite the pain of defeat, I'm still grateful for the glory of the campaign and the bond it created between my father and I. Recently, in one of life's ritual clear-out sessions, I threw away every last remnant of my childhood belongings. There was, however, one item I just couldn't discard: my 1990 World Cup sticker book. I drew a short breath when I caught sight of it, as the raw emotions all came flooding back. Over thirty years have passed, but some magic never fades.

My first trip to Elland Road was in 1992. Our primary school had fortunately managed to acquire some tickets for the FA Youth Cup Final. Teenage sensation Jamie Forrester (whose professional career ended up in the lower leagues) scored an incredible overhead kick as a triumphant Leeds United claimed the trophy with an emphatic 4–1 victory. To this day, I can still remember my disbelief at the audacity of even attempting an overhead kick, never mind actually scoring from one. As the net rippled, I couldn't believe my eyes.

The art of playing the beautiful game is revered, holy and pure. It is as much about fakery, disguise and facetiousness as it is about honesty, hard work and bravery. There are so many ways to win and lose. A simple game brimming with complexity, and the greatest topic of conversation in the known universe.

Many people have a spiritual connection with their club. Football is important — it has meaning. Yet this deep sentiment we feel towards the game, and our respective clubs, is impossible to articulate to others. As noted by Mickaël Correia in *A People's History of Football*, "for historian Eric Hobsbawm, from the 1880s onwards football embodied a 'lay religion of the British proletariat', with its church (the club), its place of worship (the stadium) and its followers (the supporters)."[1]

Football is more than just our nation's premier pastime — it's a sacred movement, woven into our very cultural identity. Furthermore, it often serves as a reflector of society's current conditions, a barometer of our country's political and economic status at any given time, and a microcosm of the thoughts and feelings of the masses.

But, alas, something is amiss. Football is in crisis. The economics that underpin it seem unsustainable: a slow-motion car crash. As early as 2011, the former UEFA President, Michel Platini, predicted disaster:

My message for football is alarming, the red lights are flashing... There is no lack of money. But it is bad financial management. We need to get rules in place... We probably won't be popular, but we have to do it. Otherwise, football will be destroyed.[2]

Despite this warning, however, there has been no major reform to football's financial model.

In order to better grasp the immensity of this predicament, we must first reflect on football's past to highlight the level of distortion that has taken hold and offer us an insight into how we can potentially wrestle back control of the game we love.

A Brief History of Football

A mass social movement that began to take shape in nineteenth-century Great Britain, football has developed into the world's most popular sport. Although similar games were seemingly played in antiquity by various cultures and civilisations, they're little more than a footnote to the real thing.

The beautiful game is said to have evolved from peasants kicking a pig's bladder between villages. Its origins are bound up in the concept of local pride. In "folk football", the goals were usually miles apart, with dozens or sometimes hundreds of spirited peasants competing on either side. Rules were limited to say the least — participants often ended up with serious injuries (or worse!). In essence, it was organised violence. The ball was more "clutched" than kicked, with players rummaging in large scrums and enjoying a few scraps in the process. Perhaps modern hooligans could claim to be merely preserving football's more traditional roots.

The ruling classes disapproved of people playing folk football as it made them less productive in the fields. Furthermore, it was often played directly through the streets of towns and villages, which often served to damage local properties. Folk football had far more in common with modern rugby and contemporary mixed martial arts than any other sports. Such was the level of violence that the game was banned on several occasions by royal decree. Nevertheless, such regal sanctions couldn't deter the people and they played regardless. After all, this was their game.

But then something changed. As Britain industrialised, land enclosures forced people out of their villages and into towns and cities of newly built factories. For the masses, as common land and leisure time began to recede, so did their traditional sporting pursuits. Along with the saint days it used to be played on, folk football began to disappear completely. The process of urbanisation chained entire families to the factory clock and left little time for anything else other than labour. In an era of tumultuous economic and social change, spanning several generations, the tradition of local peasants playing folk football freely on the commons was gradually dismantled by the onset of the Industrial Revolution. As the peasantry faced huge social upheaval and disruption, the practice of playing football then retreated into the public schools. The baton was inadvertently handed to the upper-class gentry, and it's in these educational institutions that this chaotic Mediaeval game evolved into something else entirely. Just like so many other components of Victorian society, football underwent a process of industrialisation as it became subject to strict rules and regulations.

In the nineteenth century, sport served as a tool for social control in Britain's public schools. This gave rise to the concept of "muscular Christianity", whereby pupils could cultivate a sense of moral duty and a Protestant work ethic through engagement in athletic pursuits. Team sports were actively promoted, as they were said to instil discipline and develop future leaders of Empire. As a result, an innovative and progressive ideology of athleticism emerged as a crucial element in Victorian education. Under these conditions, football thrived in its new educational setting, albeit in various forms, as each school developed its own particular set of rules.

As the nineteenth century progressed, Britain became the workshop of the world. Horrendous working conditions, overpopulated slums and periods of starvation characterised a dark chapter in the country's social history. But despite the misery inflicted upon the lower classes, this transformative era produced an array of new technologies that changed Britain forever. The mid-nineteenth century saw a network of railways spring up, significantly reducing journey times and connecting an entire nation. For the first time in history, it was possible to effortlessly travel hundreds of miles in a single day. This emerging railway network provided the catalyst for football's standardisation, and therefore its importance in the sport's primitive history should not be underestimated. Indeed, the story of two of Britain's greatest ever inventions are beautifully intertwined — the origins of the modern game run parallel to the expansion of the railways. Although the sudden ability to play teams in different areas of the country was a groundbreaking development, it also presented a major headache. The rules of the game were contingent upon where you lived, and hence there could be no uniform approach to each fixture. As public schools had formed their own codes, with some preferring scrimmaging and running with the ball in hand, which set of rules were correct? You can imagine the arguments.

To address this issue and form an apparatus of governance, on 26 October 1863 a group of Cambridge University graduates founded the Football Association (FA). One of their first tasks was to establish a standardised set of laws for what would later become known as the beautiful game. As a result of these intense meetings, some founding members withdrew from the FA immediately, completely outraged by the organisation's decision to ban some of the more physical aspects of the game. Through this development, rugby was born.

Facing resistance as many clubs and schools clung to their own codes, the FA took decisive action. In 1871, they introduced the Challenge Cup, a tournament now known as the FA Cup. The rules stipulated that each team should consist of 11 players and that matches would last for 90 minutes. This knockout competition format was ground-breaking at the time and played a contributory role towards establishing the FA's recently developed rules (one of which didn't allow you to pass forward) on a wider geographical scale.

By this stage, the first international football match had already occurred, marking the beginning of the enduring rivalry between England and Scotland in 1870. Consequently, the rules created by the newly established English FA began to permeate north of the border. Over the course of the 1870s, these rules underwent further refinement, introducing innovations such as the addition of a crossbar between the goalposts and the formulation of the offside rule. The latter initiative brought about a revolutionary change in the game, prompting a shift from individualised dribbling to a passing system reliant on collective teamwork — a tactical approach initially developed in Scotland and subsequently adopted elsewhere. Indeed, many of the early professionals were Scotsman who were offered jobs in the northwest of England in a bid to entice them to play. Scottish football appears to have peaked rather early, although a certain generation of fans who remember Archie Gemmel's iconic mazy run and neat finish against Holland may suggest otherwise.

Towards the end of the nineteenth century, social reform was creeping in, as unions started to win rights for their members. In what became a critical development, Saturday afternoons began to evolve into free time for the masses. As wages began to slowly rise and leisure time increased, football exploded, especially within industrialised working-class areas. Football may have been codified by the upper-class gentlemen of England's public schools, but, as it exploded in popularity, it did so via the working-class roots of the factory floor. It was workplaces that founded so many of our great modern football clubs, from the munitions workers of Woolwich (Arsenal) to the railway workers of Newton Heath (Manchester United).

During this period, hundreds of clubs also emerged with strong affiliations to the church. The "muscular Christianity" movement (which as we've seen was originally cultivated in public schools) was extended to the working class as the church aimed to purify society by providing young men with disciplined and structured sporting activities. With significant land ownership, the church played a major role in creating hundreds of football pitches throughout the nation. Additionally, cricket teams such as Sheffield Wednesday, Sheffield United and London-based Hotspur also began to establish football clubs as well.

Football was certainly catching on, as amateur teams sprang up around the four corners of Britain. The game provided the masses with something more than just a pastime; it gave people an identity, a piece of the world they could call their own. The psychological trauma suffered by the working class of Britain during the process of industrialisation was immense. Ripped apart from their traditional way of life, upended from the countryside and thrown into dirty urban sprawls, the masses were effectively forced into wage slavery.

However, as they continued to toil in the factories and pay rent to their landlords, they now had something that couldn't be bought or stolen. Local pride was on the agenda, and the people were claiming a new and revitalised football in order to represent their fledgling urban communities.

As the game grew, a political battle ensued for control of its future direction. It proved to be a clash of the classes. In its infancy, the FA refused to allow players to be paid, as they wanted to preserve the amateur status of the game. Nevertheless, clubs continued to search for loopholes, enticing players by disguising performance-related payments as "expenses". Realistically, whilst payment was prohibited, working-class players (who needed to earn a living) couldn't compete — a development welcomed with open arms by the upper-class gentry, who believed football should be the preserve of the rich. Public schoolboys did not intend for their sport to fall into the hands of commoners.

The battle for pay impacted footballers in the same way as it did politicians of that era who were also not compensated for their work — only the rich could afford to undertake such "amateur" pursuits. In 1885, the move towards professionalisation was finally sanctioned. The FA, predominantly composed of upper-class public school alumni, were of course reluctant to approve this transition. However, the sport's growing commercialisation was an inevitable outcome of its seemingly exponential popularity. Thousands paid to enter through the turnstiles, marking the early stages of a developing business model. Gate receipts became a source for expanding infrastructure and financing player wages. By the mid-1880s, with several teams suspended for compensating players, northern clubs threatened to establish a separate football federation. In response to this proposed rebellion, the FA yielded. Much to the dismay of the aristocrats, football was professionalised. The balance of power had shifted, and the upper-class gentry responsible for standardising the sport were usurped by a huge working-class movement from below.

Rugby remained an amateur pursuit, and so couldn't keep up with the exploding popularity of its rival. Football now had a governing body, a standardised set of rules, paid professionals, a railway network that enabled ease of travel and a growing number of very keen spectators who even sang songs in support of their favourite teams. Prestigious cup games attracted vast crowds, although attendances at friendlies were far lower. Naturally, professionalism required increased funding, so what could be done to draw in larger crowds on a more consistent basis? A revolutionary concept was in the making.

In 1888, the first football league in history was formed, containing 12 teams from the industrial heartlands of Lancashire and the Midlands. It's interesting to note the lack of southern teams. Indeed, professional football was very much established in the northern industrial powerhouses. The aristocrats of the south managed to keep "their" football as an amateur pursuit for a few years after 1888, but it wouldn't stay that way for long. This north/south divide had also been seen in rugby, resulting in the formation of two completely different codes. Thankfully, the beautiful game survived intact.

Only a few generations earlier, the landed gentry had stolen football through fencing off the commons and significantly decreasing leisure time for the masses. However, by the time Queen Victoria had entered the closing stages of her reign, the working class, direct descendants of a repressed peasantry, had taken it back. In doing so, they helped define not only modern football, but also their own sense of self within these new urbanised surroundings. Essentially, the origins of modern football are defined by class warfare, a dynamic still very much prevalent in today's game, particularly in relation to a football club's ownership model.

The late Victorian period presided over the foundation of many of our great football clubs, built by the working class, for the working class. In 1893, the Second Division was added as the professional pyramid began to expand. This newly established game grew exponentially; never before had a sport become so popular, so quickly. During the inaugural 1888/89 season, there was a total of 602,000 paying spectators; by the mid-1890s, this figure had risen to almost 2 million.[3] People had less leisure time and less money than they do today, yet football was still accessible and affordable to the masses: it truly was the people's game.

In the aftermath of WWI, many spectator sports saw an increase in viewing numbers, and football was no exception. During the early 1920s, Division Three was added (in a two-league regional format), as the fledgling footballing pyramid began to take shape. The most successful teams attracted the biggest crowds. A formidable Arsenal side drew in the most spectators during the 1930s, before Newcastle United claimed the highest attendances in the immediate post-war period.

In many respects, the late 1940s and early 1950s were a golden age for English football. Much loved players, such as Stanley Mathews, were etching their names into footballing immortality as a traumatised nation began to recover from the horrors of total war. Overall average attendances (throughout all divisions) were the highest in history. Nationwide, the terraces were packed. For all the glitz and glamour of the modern game, there is a different type of connection to football that has been diminished. For a prolonged period, fans have been far less inclined to leave their sofas and attend local football matches. The television screen has brought football into our homes, and as a result we have made less of an effort to go out and watch it. Technological advancements don't just impact the football industry, they reshape it and redefine it completely in a continuous process. The way in which fandom relates to the beautiful game is in a constant state of flux, now more so than ever, but our passion for it has never wavered, and its roots run deep into our past. For well over a century, the rituals of football have been of crucial importance to the people of this nation. The baby boomers were born into communities that sang songs inside packed stadiums, and we still sing those very songs today.

It's important to understand what our Victorian forebears created for themselves, and in turn for us, their generational descendants. This game is more than just merely entertainment, and a football club is nothing less than an institution. As Rachel Botsman states in *Who Can You Trust?*:

> We often think of institutions as something physical — grand university buildings, ancient stone churches, The Houses of Parliament — but they can also be an idea, a constraint, or a social norm. Marriage is an institution, so is the family unit or the British monarchy. You know when you are inside one, just as a bee knows when it is in the hive. In other words, concrete or conceptual, they are valued building blocks of rule and repetition on which society is built. They shape our behaviour and how we interact with one another.[4]

A football club embodies Botsman's description of an institution perfectly. It's a powerful idea, one that binds us together, a social norm, and a hive in which we belong. We know when we're inside it.

But what do our footballing history books conspire to teach us? Why is the history of football so important to the central objective of this book? The answer is simple. Football is nothing without its founding principles, its working-class roots and its wholesome position in the local community. The happiness of one's locality is often chiefly contingent upon the performance of its football club. What other sport, movement or dynamic can profess to hold such weight?

Football clubs were initially created to represent something that exists outside the realm of soulless, profit-driven monetisation. It's because of this that they have survived generations, carefully handed down intact, whilst, in wider society, big businesses and corporations collapsed around them. Our football clubs were formed separate to the capitalist model and built to represent those who had no voice. Although they exemplify the British love of sporting pursuits, they're just as much about social bonding as they are about kicking leather. Essentially, the very essence of what a football club really is can be summarised as an institution immersed in pride. People often bond with them to celebrate locality, but their message is universal: we matter.

The Tragic Truth of Today

Our football clubs, formed as sovereign, independent, working-class institutions, have over the last few decades been fenced off from the public and now belong to a wealthy elite. As a result, they're now run purely as business ventures. Profit margins come first, and fans come last. This has eaten away at notions of loyalty and romance and undermined deep emotional connections. Ultimately, our clubs are being systematically destroyed via profiteering. Previous generations of fandom had not been subjected to this cultural shift and viewed football through a different lens, one that had a closer relationship to notions of community, sportsmanship, fair play and integrity.

It's important to understand that, for over a century, football was governed differently. Our ancestors realised a basic truth that we have forgotten in today's frantic world of rampant consumerism: the pursuit of profit isn't everything. This is a wisdom that now evades us, as we've been severed from our past.

In an increasingly globalised world, billionaire investors have taken the structure of our proud heritage and shaken it to the very core, remoulding it to suit their own agendas. In such a reality, only winners matter, and the rest are rendered worthless. This sentiment has worrying implications for the future of the beautiful game. As always, the innate wisdom of Marcelo Bielsa holds true:

> The commercialisation of football when clubs are owned by private people makes the result more important than anything… But the most attractive thing in football is the beauty of the game. Those who invest in football should be aware of that and take precautions to protect the business they bought. The fact that we are not taking care of the planet, our children will pay the consequences of our acts. And with football it will be the same because we are destroying football. And in the future, we will see the negative effects of this.[5]

An aggressive process of commercialisation is continuing to impact our national game, taking it further and further away from its working-class roots. Power dynamics have long since shifted. Unfortunately, there is little resistance being offered. In the present day, we — the people of the people's game — are divided and directionless. It's fair to suggest that club owners do not always share the same interests as us supporters. But at the clubs where this contradiction has flared up most acutely, fanbases have tended to turn their anger upon lone individuals, rather than addressing the systemic cause of the issue. Too distracted by on-field matters and a never-ending media circus, we prefer the sanctuary of our own club's bubble.

If we are to reclaim our game, just as our Victorian ancestors did, then we'll need to collectively mobilise around matters off the pitch. Surely, the time has come for us to stop passing the buck and convene on a much wider scale. The question is: what type of change do we (the supporters) want? However, before that question can be answered with any degree of confidence, we must first understand the process of our dispossession.

The Neoliberal Takeover

The ideology of neoliberalism, with its privatisation, its deregulation, its emphasis on consumption, its elimination of basically any apparatuses that can provide alternative points of view, has been so powerful and so normalised.

Henry Giroux

In response to the recent development of players taking the knee prior to kick off, some social commentators suggested that we should "keep politics out of football". It's vital here that we address a common misconception — politics is *already* in football. The way in which football is governed, (un)regulated and financially structured is deeply political, and blatantly undemocratic.

For the best part of a century, the FA had a pivotal piece of legislation which defined how clubs were run. Rule 34 determined that no individual could extract profit from the endeavours of a football club. This was principally a safeguarding measure, protecting football clubs from greedy profiteers, meaning that a club was managed in the interests of the local community that sustained it. You won't be surprised to learn that Rule 34 is no longer adhered to, and our football clubs are now forced to pursue an entirely different agenda.

So what are the origins of Rule 34? Football journalist David Conn has researched this matter extensively and his work provides an interesting overview. For Conn, the key club is Preston North End:

> In 1892, the FA permitted Preston North End, football's first great power, to convert itself from a members' club into a limited company. Preston had, years earlier, been the first to break the rules against professionalism, paying good players from Scotland to come to the club at a time when paying players was still illicit. The club's application to form a company was partly to raise new money, partly to limit its members' personal liability for the increased operating expenses. The FA decreed in 1892 that a club could make itself into a company, but that dividends to shareholders must be restricted. Here was the basis for football's future development: the clubs became businesses, which could pay players, build grounds, charge supporters for entry, and form themselves into companies. But the FA insisted they remain clubs in their culture. The supporter's gut feeling that the club is a collective endeavour, an organisation he belongs to, not a company seeking profit for shareholders, was embedded in the regulations. Rule 34, requiring football club-companies to be run essentially as non-profit organisations, with their directors serving as "custodians", was in the FA handbook until the late 1990s.[1]

Football clubs may well be limited companies, but they're not supposed to be run in the interests of shareholders. First and foremost, they are community assets. Rule 34 stated that directors are "custodians" of a football club and prohibited them from taking a salary from club-generated funds. It also prevented dividends from being rewarded to shareholders. In later years the regulation was relaxed, but the percentage awarded to shareholders was still capped. Holding directorship of a football club was essentially a duty to the local community, more akin to a public service than running a standard business.

In football's fledgling years, tens of thousands clicked through the turnstiles to watch their teams play. Indeed, professional football has always generated significant revenue streams, and this has positioned it firmly within the classic dimensions of the business realm. However, Rule 34 ensured that club culture was maintained and that the game belonged firmly in the hands of the people. This fine balance lasted generations, as football's financial landscape was strictly regulated. Player wages were capped, gate receipts were shared between clubs and matchday tickets were kept cheap.

In the post-war period, football remained affordable to the masses, although player wages soon began to inflate. Jimmy Hill spearheaded a successful campaign in the 1950s, which resulted in the lifting of the wage cap in 1961. Prior to this, salaries had been restricted to a paltry £20 a week. Suddenly, as wages began to increase, so did the value of the transfer market. Manchester United legend (and Leeds United teenage reject) George Best was the first player to be paid £1,000 a week. Thanks to Jimmy Hill, the most talented players now came with a hefty price tag. The wage cap that was implemented in the 1950s was absurdly low, and it was rightfully challenged. However, banishing it entirely helped sow the seeds for the opposite problem: hyper-wage inflation.

The late 1970s welcomed another financial milestone: Trevor Francis became the first £1 million transfer. Even without the colossal TV contracts of the modern era, football was still generating large amounts of revenue. Come the early 1980s, these developments hadn't gone unnoticed. The metaphorical vultures of high finance were circling, and their political and economic philosophies would soon become a hallmark of the game they intruded upon. Neoliberalism descended upon football, and with it came grave repercussions for fans. The circumventing of Rule 34 is evidence that we have been completely hoodwinked. So, how (and when) did our protective legislation disappear?

The Ideological Shift

Neoliberalism is an economic philosophy which champions the right of the individual above the well-being of the collective. Favouring free market policies, deregulation and reduced government spending, it limits the capacity of the state through a process of privatisation and austerity.

To understand how the ideology of neoliberalism infiltrated and defined the modern game, it's worth reflecting on the wider political landscape. In particular, we need to take note of a shift in the perceived centre ground of political thought, otherwise known as "the Overton Window", that occurred between the late 1970s and early 1980s. After a period of economic decline which culminated in the 1978 Winter of Discontent, the social contract of post-war Britain was cast aside and in its place came neoliberalism, as Margaret Thatcher exploited the chaos created by a financial crisis and offered Britain a clear alternative. In tandem with US president Ronald Reagan, Thatcher proposed a fiscal programme that would reduce state intervention, slash regulation and encourage the privatisation of the public sphere. Her belief in the "invisible hand" of globalised markets was absolute, and her ruthlessness in crushing rebellious labour movements earned her a new title, The Iron Lady (there were also other names she was known by).

Although perhaps not a well-documented development, Margaret Thatcher's impact on football was colossal. The rise of Thatcherism represented a shift in the pervasive common sense. Mindsets had been altered — protective regulation was now seen as restrictive and regressive. In Thatcher's eyes, the power and freedom of the affluent individual should not be curtailed because, according to her at least, there was "no such thing as society". An era of individualism had begun, pre-empting the dawn of a new economic order.

The general consensus is that 1992 — the year the Premier League was established — represents the biggest economic changepoint in English football in the modern era. However, 1983 was arguably even more impactful. This was the year Tottenham Hotspur chairman Irving Scholar wrote to the FA and informed them that he intended to flout Rule 34. When the FA didn't even bother to respond, Irving went ahead with laying the groundwork for an aggressive commercialisation plan, establishing a separate commercial enterprise tethered to Tottenham Hotspur. This enabled funds to be funnelled from the "parent businesses" into a subsidiary holding company. Suddenly, the conditions for direct profit extraction from a football club had been realised. With this act, English football was changed forever. Irving's holding company model meant that shares in a football club could be bought and sold for private profit, without prohibitive regulation getting in the way.

Perhaps the main reason that Rule 34 was flouted at this particular juncture was the development of lucrative broadcasting contracts. For the first time, at the beginning of the 1983/84 season, regular live football league fixtures were aired via ITV and the BBC. With the two biggest broadcasters now competing for contracts and pumping money into the industry, millions of pounds would be up for grabs and control of monetary flow was paramount — protective legislation needed to go, or at least be ignored.

In yet another change to our footballing discourse, 1983 also saw the scrapping of shared gate receipts, and away teams would no longer get an equal cut of matchday ticket sales. The bigger clubs were beginning to put more pressure on the traditional structures of governance, regardless of how it impacted everyone else — a pattern that has continued to play out ever since.

The Decline of English Football

The abandonment of Rule 34 was not only a watershed moment in the economics of football, it also coincided with a period of decline both on and off the pitch. Hooliganism spiralled out of control. Violence in and around stadiums became commonplace, with native football fans gaining a reputation for thuggery and aggression. Matchday clashes with police became routine, and stadiums began to look increasingly like prisons, as high fences emerged from concrete terraces in an attempt to control the hostility.

A small network of football hooligans initiated a circus of destruction wherever they went, grabbing the headlines and providing a perfect smokescreen for the neoliberal boardroom takeover. After the Heysel Disaster in 1985 (a partial stadium collapse which resulted in 39 deaths), Margaret Thatcher declared in a press interview that, "We have to get the game cleaned up from this hooliganism at home and then perhaps we shall be able to go overseas again".[2] In response, the FA imposed a five-year ban on English teams, prohibiting their participation in any European competitions. It was a hammer blow, as English football's reign of European dominance throughout the late Seventies and early Eighties came to an abrupt end.

In 1989, English football then suffered a tragedy that continues to haunt the city of Liverpool to this day. At Hillsborough, an unsafe stadium, coupled with incompetent policing, resulted in the unlawful deaths of 96 innocent people. A 97th victim, who sustained life-changing injuries because of the incident, died over 32 years later. In the aftermath of this heartbreaking afternoon, the *Sun* newspaper wrongly (and vindictively) blamed the Liverpool supporters in attendance. Questions of accountability remain unanswered; justice is still being sought.

Being banned from Europe, with violence inside stadiums and ongoing enquiries into the standards of policing on matchdays, English football's reputation was in tatters. A sporting rebrand was desperately needed. As a result of the Hillsborough disaster, Lord Justice Taylor recommended that every stadium in England's top two tiers become all-seater. Naturally, the question of funding for this renovation arose, and the Labour Party in opposition advocated for utilising public funds. They pointed to the substantial tax revenues generated by football pools, totalling £250 million annually,[3] suggesting that this income could be allocated to finance the entire renovation project. However, in January 1990, the proposal was rejected in Parliament. The ruling Tory party had other plans, as football was thrust deeper into the private sphere. Instead, clubs would be expected to fund the transition to all-seater stadiums independently by cashing in on more lucrative broadcasting deals.[4] The foundations of the Premier League were being forged in a perfect storm.

The Birth of the Premier League

The creation of the Premier League ran parallel to the Champions League rebrand — the timing of these events was not coincidental. By the new division's launch in 1992, Western capitalism's victory over Soviet communism was fully complete and the regulatory shackles were off. Rule 34 had already been abandoned and the power dynamic was shifting as the biggest clubs demanded more, and the smallest braced themselves for hardship.

An era of bold and expansive big business replaced the so-called "backward" ideology of regulatory constraints. Amidst this new landscape, a small group of businessmen were about to force the agenda. The owners of Liverpool, Everton, Manchester United, Arsenal and Tottenham Hotspur had a new commercial strategy in mind, one that looked to enhance sponsorship rights and redirect far greater revenues into the bank accounts of the biggest clubs. This new commercial strategy was to be largely financed by a controversial overseas investor.

At the turn of the 1990s, Rupert Murdoch's BSKYB was losing vast amounts of money. Consumers weren't interested in paying for the cinema services it offered and the Australian media mogul found himself in huge amounts of debt. He decided to take a gamble on English football. England's 1990 World Cup campaign, in which twenty-five million people tuned in to watch the semi-final defeat to Germany, provided sufficient evidence to Murdoch that our love of the game could be monetised. A communal and emotive sporting event is an advertiser's dream and the boardroom at BSKYB clearly took note.

The British television industry was already in the process of being marketised. The Broadcasting Act of 1990 granted

Rupert Murdoch a significant political favour by liberating BSKYB from the regulatory restrictions applied to terrestrial broadcasters. However, the Labour opposition leader, Neil Kinnock, wanted to bring this suspicious deal before the Mergers and Monopoly Commission, which posed a serious problem to Murdoch's clear monopolisation agenda.[5] The 1992 general election proved to be a significant turning point — the Tories pulled off an unexpected victory and Neil Kinnock's threat was quashed. As a result, the Australian was gifted full right of passage.

There were controversial aspects to Murdoch's rebranding — the new league launched with cheerleaders, for one — but it was a process that was always framed as progress. Millions signed up, accessing live football on a Sunday afternoon and Monday night. Murdoch saw an opportunity and exploited a crisis. His inspiration was Silvio Berlusconi, the controversial Italian businessman and politician who was the first to recognise the potential of selling football matches to a wider TV audience and had already facilitated the beaming of Serie A into UK television sets every weekend. The commercialisation of sport was evolving. Cable and satellite TV technologies had arrived and consumers were demanding more and more live football on their increasingly large television screens.

The old, tarnished English First Division was out, and the new, improved and far more fashionable Premier League was in. Everything had conspired in favour of Murdoch's dream, allowing his empire to make vast amounts of money whilst maintaining his influence in the corridors of power. In 1992–93, Murdoch's bold and ambitious scheme provided the Premier League with a huge cash injection, and this commercial juggernaut has continued to expand ever since.

Mind the Gap

In many respects, the Premier League has been a massive success. However, this has come at a hefty price to the consumer, who is now expected to pay a range of different companies for the privilege of watching live football. To add insult to injury, swathes of English fandom have been priced out of their local stadium on matchday, unable to afford the rising fees. There is also another price to pay for those who seek a more meaningful or spiritual connection with football — the growing distance between club and supporter.

The privatisation of our football clubs could be compared with the land enclosures of the sixteenth century onwards — they have been fenced off from the communities that built them and turned into the private property of a wealthy landowner. Through efforts in 2009, and again in 2011, a collection of Arsenal FC shareholders gained around £300 million when they sold their stake in the club to American businessman Stan Kroenke. This money was sucked out of Arsenal FC and filtered into the pockets of wealthy individuals. Such an example of shareholder dealings serves to highlight the fact that this is no longer the financial model our predecessors preserved. Those who originally invested in Arsenal did not extract profit for personal gain, as the system forbade it. But, evidently, systems can change. Since the 1980s, our biggest football clubs have been allowed to pursue economic policies which prioritise their own lust for greed over anything else. As a result, in an era defined by huge broadcasting deals, the vast majority of revenue has been sucked to the very top of the pyramid.

Rise of the Monopolies

Greed, in the end, fails even the greedy.

Cathryn Louis

One of the most telling consequences of neoliberalism's economic doctrine is the creation of domineering monopolies. In football, this means that wealth, power and influence all become increasingly concentrated into a small number of "super clubs". This is a self-perpetuating cycle which ensures that these elite clubs grow continuously stronger. Consequently, fair competition is undermined and a predictable pattern of winners has emerged in England and beyond. Although some elite-level fixtures still manage to produce unexpected results, these occasions are becoming rarer and rarer.

This is not to say that the game doesn't need powerful clubs. We all enjoy the spectacle of watching an incredible team packed with world-class talent and a super-sized fanbase cheering them on. Moreover, the ever-romantic notion of David vs Goliath plays a significant role in our footballing discourse — an underdog creates a more compelling narrative. However, we've arrived at a tipping point: David's hands are being tied behind his back. However, it could be argued that today's modern monopolies no longer even represent Goliath; they're morphing into unbeatable God-like entities who won't even allow David the opportunity to challenge them.

The proposed European Super League (ESL) is the latest expression of this monopolistic agenda. According to James Plunkett, a monopoly is "a firm that dominates a market so fully that they break free from the constraints of competition".[1] This is often achieved via mergers and acquisitions — powerful businesses combining under one umbrella to control the market — which is exactly what 12 football clubs attempted to do under the guise of the ESL. This should come as no surprise — in an economic structure that paves the way for "super clubs" to corner the market and become permanent winners of everything, the formation of a European Super League is the next natural step to take, entrenching existing power structures and eradicating the threat of relegation. With competition effectively over, super clubs could then further consolidate power, influence and earnings.

To understand the origins of the ESL, we once again turn to Silvio Berlusconi. After buying AC Milan in 1986, he set about commercialising his investment, declaring that "Milan is a team, but it is also something to sell; something to offer on the market".[2] His approach had far-reaching consequences. It was then that Berlusconi first suggested the idea of a European Super League. He had been broadcasting football domestically since 1980 and was the first to recognise the true power of international television rights as live Italian football was beamed across the globe in the early 1990s. This is where Murdoch got his inspiration, building upon Berlusconi's pioneering broadcasting model.

Premier League teams received a combined £61 million in the 1992/93 season, triggering the beginnings of a huge competitive advantage. Those outside the top flight were excluded. It could be argued that this very transaction represented the start of the end for fair competition, and since then the gap between the Premier League and the rest of the pyramid has only continued to widen. In 1993/94 and 1994/95, newly promoted sides to the Premier League finished in third place (Newcastle United and Nottingham Forest, respectively). In today's footballing landscape, a newly promoted side could never dream of attaining such dizzying heights. The last time a newly promoted club even finished inside the top five was Ipswich Town in 2000/01.

Furthermore, the money pumped into the top division has been far from evenly divided, with the so-called "bigger clubs" receiving a far larger slice of the cake. One of football's leading financial experts, Kieran Maguire, has broken down payments made to Premier League clubs from commercial TV rights. The annual reports from the 2021/22 season (latest figures available at the time of writing) provide a snapshot of a process which serves to create huge inequalities. For example, Liverpool was given a staggering £159 million more than Norwich City. The three highest earners in that season received a combined total of £745 million, a difference of £435 million compared with the combined total of the three lowest earners.

However, these figures only account for broadcasting revenue. Add in the huge gulf in sponsorship monies, match day attendance profits, merchandise sales and Champions League payments, and the gap widens enormously. With Financial Fair Play (FFP) guidelines ensuring that clubs spend within their means (thus ceding an advantage to richer clubs), football's current economic cycle condemns our game to inevitability.

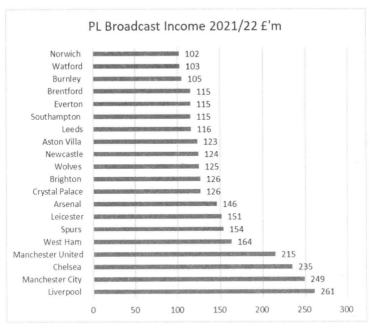

Figures taken from the annual reports of each of the Premier League clubs

The Wealthiest Just Keep Winning

When it comes to the distribution of income generated via broadcasting, the status quo argues that the "big six" are pulling in the largest TV audiences and are therefore entitled to the most money. This has been the basic premise of the Premier League's broadcasting model ever since Murdoch entered the fray. Tottenham Hotspur's Daniel Levy has doubled down on this sentiment, claiming that he and his club "only want what's fair". Perhaps his notion of "fair" is a slightly warped one. As more and more money has been pumped into the English top tier and syphoned off to the biggest teams, the league's competitive nature has diminished. It's worth noting that when broadcasting money first entered the footballing landscape in 1965, it was shared evenly amongst all 92 teams. From a modern perspective, such an egalitarian approach to financial distribution feels consigned to the history books.

To best demonstrate the relentless growth of monopolisation in the modern game, we can examine long-term trends. The erosion of competition reveals itself most clearly in the total number of points accrued by recent title winners when compared to previous eras. During the 1990s, when the monopolisation process was at a less advanced stage, title challengers generally weren't as dominant over the rest of the league. In a thrilling four-horse title race, the 1996/97 season saw Manchester United take first spot with just 75 points. The following year, Arsenal secured their first ever Premier League title after tallying a modest 78 points. During the 1998/99 campaign, Manchester United's treble-winning champion team claimed the trophy back, finishing the season on 79 points. How do these statistics compare to the modern day?

Although there are some standout seasons, the overall trend is clear. On average, in the first ten years of the Premier League (figure adjusted for a 38-game season), a team could win the title on 80 points (2.1 points per game). During the second decade of the Premier League's existence, that figure rose to 87 points (2.3 points per game). In the third decade, the average number of points for title winners hit 91 (2.4 points per game). Leicester City's remarkable title victory in 2015/16 represents a glitch in the monopolisation process — the machine malfunctioned, allowing a supposedly relegation-threatened side to claim the title with just 81 points. However, in the seven seasons after Leicester City's triumph, the average number of points needed to win the Premier League rose to 94 (2.5 points per game). Perhaps this is a sign of things to come. The monopolisation process may not be immune to glitches, but it certainly responds to them effectively.

The concentration of points at the higher end of the Premier League table has become a ridiculous feature of contemporary top-flight competition. Liverpool gained 97 points during the 2018/19 campaign, and still didn't end the season as champions. The year before, Manchester City had become the first ever side to reach the century mark, averaging 2.6 points per game, a feat nearly matched two years later when Liverpool lifted the title after recording 99 points. Manchester City claimed the 2021/22 Premier League trophy by collecting 93 points, second-placed Liverpool could only manage 92. During the 2022/23 campaign, Arsenal reached 50 points at the halfway stage but were unable to continue their rich vein of form as Manchester City collected the title for the fifth time in six seasons. City may have only tallied a below-par 89 points, but they dropped five points in the last two games due to fielding weakened teams, with the title already mathematically secured and a Champions League final on the horizon. History was made the following year when Manchester City became champions of England for an unprecedented fourth season in a row. The Citizens were pushed all the way for the title, claiming it with a familiar total in the monopolisation process — 91 points.

Although there may be some seasons that buck the trend, gradually, over time, this financial system has created "a league within a league", where only the richest teams can battle it out for the title. There is a direct correlation between a club's spending power and on-field success. Leicester City's remarkable season of 2015/16 has been the only major anomaly to the monopolisation process and could well be the final time that such disruption to the new order occurs. Unsurprisingly, that title-winning team was torn apart by wealthier clubs, including the immediate departure to Chelsea FC of midfield maestro N'Golo Kante, who then picked up the league title with his new club the following season.

Seven different clubs were crowned Premier League champions during the first 30 years of its existence. How does this figure compare with previous eras? Since 1888 there have been 125 competitive seasons in the English top flight. Therefore, a 30-year timescale can be applied to represent roughly one-quarter of our entire competitive league format. If we focus on the 30 seasons prior to the Premier League era (1962/63–1991/92), then one club stands out as being a dominating force: Liverpool lifted the trophy on 13 different occasions throughout this period. However, despite one side winning nearly half the titles, we still see nine different clubs winning the league during this quarter, an increase of two when compared to the Premier League era.

If we consider the next batch of 30 competitive seasons (1925/26–1961/62), then the difference is stark. Throughout this quarter of English football's history, no less than 15 different clubs managed to win the title — a huge increase. This figure is nearly matched in the first quarter of our competitive top-flight history, from 1888/89–1924/25 (a period of 32 seasons), when 13 different clubs reached the pinnacle of English football. This leaves us in little doubt that the English game is becoming less and less competitive. The first two quarters saw an average of 14 different club sides winning the league, whereas it drops to an average of just 8 in the second two quarters. This clear long-term trend is amplified even further when we scrutinise the number of Premier League winners more closely: over 90% of league titles have been won by just four teams.

The monopolisation process also reveals itself in football's oldest competition, the FA Cup. Throughout its long history, underdogs have certainly had their fair share of magical days. From 1973 to 1980, there were three instances of second-tier teams lifting the trophy. My first footballing memory extends all the way back to 1988, when Vinnie Jones and his Crazy Gang unexpectedly beat Liverpool in the final. However, in the 36 seasons after Wimbledon's FA Cup glory, the "big six" have triumphed on no less than 32 occasions (89%).

A similar pattern is playing out in the EFL Cup. It began in 1961, and throughout the first three decades of its existence there were five instances of second-tier teams lifting the trophy. But in the Premier League era — a period of 32 seasons — only top-tier sides have prevailed, with the "big six" claiming victory on 24 occasions (75%). At first glance, the EFL Cup appears to be more competitive. However, the undeniable trend towards monopoly rears its head when we consider the previous 20 seasons in isolation. Since Middlesborough's victory in 2004, the "big six" have lifted the EFL Cup on 18 occasions (90%).

The Pyramid Is Crumbling

This sustained upward mobility of wealth for the Premier League's various stakeholders has had huge implications for those outside the top flight. Since the 1992/93 season, there has been a consistent, year-on-year increase to the volume of money flowing into the top division of the pyramid, with the annual figure now exceeding £3 billion. This represents more than a 5,000% rise within a 30-year timeframe.

The Premier League has no obligation to support the leagues below it, so it doesn't bother to. However, parachute payments are given to its relegated teams, thus offering them a huge competitive advantage over the other second-tier sides. In the 2021/22 season, the combined cost of all Championship squads amounted to £1.19 billion. Over one-third of that total stemmed from just two clubs — Fulham and Bournemouth — both beneficiaries of Premier League parachute payments.[3] Rather predictably, these were the two teams that gained automatic promotion back into the top flight. As this monopolisation process matures, it becomes increasingly likely that a relegated team will gain promotion the following season (and vice versa).

Nevertheless, the 2023/24 Championship season still managed to produce an unexpected glitch. The three beneficiaries of fresh parachute payments — Leicester City, Leeds United and Southampton — ended up finishing in first, third and fourth place respectively. The second automatic promotion spot went to Ipswich Town, who ended the season on 96 points. To achieve such a high points tally with only a modest wage bill is incredible — Kieran McKenna's triumphant Tractor Boys certainly defied the odds. But how long can they keep doing so? The gap between the best and the rest has widened significantly since Town's previous promotion to the top tier at the turn of the century. In 2024/25, mere survival is the only realistic goal for any newly promoted Premier League team: the previous season saw Sheffield United, Burnley and Luton Town all relegated straight back into the Championship.

Financially speaking, England's second tier is not a great place to be. In 2022, the combined net debt of Championship clubs reached £1.65 billion, with wage bills often exceeding revenue.[4] In 2023, Zal Udwadia, Assistant Director of Deloitte's

Sports Business Group said, "From a wages point of view, this is now the fifth year in a row that the wage-to-revenue ratio is above 100% for the Championship, which is quite concerning".[5] In a perilous financial landscape, club owners gamble recklessly whilst attempting to reach the promised land of the Premier League.

In a span of over a century, starting from the formation of the first professional league in 1888 and concluding with the end of the First Division era in 1992, there were very few instances of clubs going into administration. Since the establishment of the Premier League, in just over 30 years, there have been over 60. It appears that financial meltdown is an accelerating trend. Prior to the formation of the Premier League, cases of administration were rare; the rate is now over two per season. Easter Island economics.

Our historic pyramid structure is rapidly crumbling before our very eyes. Recently, Bury and Macclesfield were liquidated, whilst a host of other clubs continue to flirt with financial peril. A significant portion of clubs competing in the three leagues below the Premiership have faced winding-up petitions in recent years. An economic framework which asserts increasing amounts of financial pressure upon clubs residing outside of the top flight means that the internal business strategies of lower league clubs need to be extremely well-planned and executed. Otherwise, disaster may strike. Owners who make incompetent financial decisions could ultimately end up putting the club's very survival in jeopardy. There is no safety net.

Macclesfield Town went out of business with a debt of around £500,000, a sum which wouldn't even cover some elite players' weekly wage.[6] Institutions that have lasted hundreds of years dissolve in the blink of an eye, and with them goes a sense of heritage, culture and tradition. Furthermore, this relatively recent cycle of misery and destruction shows no sign of abating. Inequality is a necessary by-product of the neoliberal vision. Communities, galvanised by their local football club, become direct victims of this systematic failure.

To compound the misery further, this financial model also facilitates huge amounts of debt amongst the elite club monopolies. The combined debt of the 12 teams that signed up to the ESL was £5.6 billion — hence their urgency to establish the competition. Moreover, despite vast revenue streams channelling their way towards the English top flight, the total amount of club debt within the Premier League equates to billions of pounds.[7] Evidently, this neoliberalised economic structure ensures that virtually every football club finds itself laden with huge levels of debt, no matter where they are in the pyramid.

But how has fandom reacted to the rise of modern monopolies? Are there any long-term trends that show our direction of travel? The lifeblood of any football club is the local community it exists to represent, but how many people in these jurisdictions are now buying in to the elite-club monopolies instead? A simple comparison of club revenues clearly indicates that we are choosing to place our money into these monopolies at the expense of our local clubs.

This sentiment washes through when comparing historical attendance figures. Rounded to the nearest whole thousand, in the decade 2010 to 2020, the average top-tier crowd was 36,000, whereas the average fourth tier attendance was 4,000 — a ratio of 9:1. During the first decade of the fourth tier's existence (1959 to 1969), the average attendance of the top-flight was 29,000, versus a typical fourth tier gate of 6,000 — a ratio of less than 5:1.[8] Clearly, presence at fourth-tier football fixtures has reduced dramatically since the 1960s. From this, we can infer that the spirit and culture of our native fandom has evolved, with support migrating towards "bigger clubs" and less emphasis being placed on geographical location. The glamour of televised Premier League football has come at a cost to the rest of the pyramid, summarily altering the habits of the "average" football fan. We aren't as concerned with watching our local team anymore because we can experience all the top-flight drama from the comfort of our own living room.

A revolution in communication technologies has changed the wider footballing landscape, reshaping culture, fandom and the economic structure that underpins the game. In the modern era, if a player reaches a certain standard, there is a general expectation that they must move to a "big club". Even Premier League stalwarts such as Aston Villa, West Ham and Everton can't keep hold of their most talented local lads anymore. Should a manager or coach develop a good reputation, then the general consensus is that they "deserve a chance at a top club". This trend has revealed itself on a global scale. The result? All the world's best players and coaches are being sucked into a tiny network of European-based super clubs.

All across the continent, these clubs outspend opposition and win their domestic titles virtually every season: Juventus and the Milan clubs in Italy, Bayern in Germany, Salzburg in Austria, PSG in France, Real Madrid and Barcelona in Spain — the list goes on. Obviously, this monopolisation process has impacted European football's most prestigious competition. The 1992 Champions League rebrand may have opened the door for more clubs to compete, but the format hasn't exactly worked out well for underdogs. During the 1980s, ranked outsiders such as Nottingham Forest, Hamburger SV and Steaua Bucureşti all won the European Cup. In 1990/91, Red Star Belgrade were crowned champions. But since the formation of the Champions League, such unexpected victories have been completely wiped from the map. Marseille's success in 1992/93, Ajax's victory in 1994/95 and Porto's triumph in 2003/04 are the only occasions when the Champions League hasn't been won by clubs competing in Europe's top four leagues (England, Spain, Germany and Italy). At the time of writing, 75% of Champions League trophies have been shared by just seven teams. The European Super League is already here in everything but name.

The Future of Football

When studying history, it's rather convenient to assume that all of its outcomes were obvious and inevitable, as that is how they're usually presented to us. But this simply isn't the case. History is littered with twists and turns that few saw coming. Nevertheless, it would be difficult to argue that football's current economic landscape isn't facilitating the continued rise of the monopolies.

By following the monopolisation process through to its natural conclusion, forecasts can be suitably made about the future of the wider footballing pyramid. It's difficult to create a timeframe for the following predictions, but if preventative action is not taken to reverse the process of monopolisation, then the following scenarios become increasingly more likely to occur:

- Competition throughout Europe's top leagues will continue to erode as a select number of teams dominate proceedings and a European Super League (ESL) will naturally evolve. Ironically, this will be seen as "progress" by some fans, who've grown weary of the current structure's lack of competitiveness.

- This new European competition will become world football's central focus, growing in influence and eventually morphing into a continent-wide domestic league in its own right. The financial implications for the Premier League (and other European top flight divisions) will be dire. Monies collected from sponsorship and TV rights will naturally decrease, creating huge amounts of financial pressure.
- The "super clubs" of the ESL will remain active in their respective domestic leagues. However, their participating sides will take on a B-team status. Domestic leagues will essentially exist to cultivate future ESL first-team players.
- All powerful ESL clubs may begin to merge/partner with other competing domestic clubs, offering financial support in exchange for control of player contracts, meaning that all domestic clubs will essentially become feeder teams for ESL giants.
- Eventually, because of the overwhelming desire to generate more and more money and consolidate power, ESL monopolies will partner with Asian and American equivalents to form an all-powerful World Super League. Clubs would be truly global in nature with various home stadiums dotted all over the world.

Locality matters not in a business model fixated on globalisation. The practice of moving a football club's location has already been achieved in England with MK Dons, a development that helpless Wimbledon fans were powerless to stop, as their club relocated from south London to Milton

Keynes. The art of switching a club's location has also been seen in American football, where the St Louis Rams were moved from Missouri to Los Angeles — concerningly, the individual behind this switch was no other than Stan Kroenke, the current owner of Arsenal.

Supporters of ESL clubs may find their teams playing some home games off this island. Britain is a small and saturated market in a world full of potential riches. Expansion into new markets is the economic rule, and with their huge populations of consumers, Asia and North America would be of particular interest to super clubs looking to plant roots deeper into foreign territories.

By their very nature, monopolies will never stand still. They must grow, dominate and totally eradicate any form of competition, hence the "closed shop" model of the ESL. As it stands, all roads lead to monopolisation, and this is the want of the economic system that is currently being employed in football, or rather, is now *employing* football.

With a captive audience totalling billions of people across the globe, a Super League structure would provide the perfect environment for giant multinationals to maximise profits. Therefore it would make sense for massive corporations to purchase ownership rights to elite clubs. Indeed, this potential trend has already begun its ascent. The energy drink Red Bull has recently invested in German, Austrian and US clubs, and of course renamed these entities for branding purposes. Constantly paying for advertising seems pointless when buying a club outright will ensure you can advertise free of charge. Could we soon see the likes of Amazon, Apple or Google moving into the footballing realm as club owners? They certainly have the capital necessary to purchase and develop a club's infrastructure, and actively partaking in the world's most popular sport would offer them unique opportunities for harnessing soft power and influencing public opinion.

It may seem a far-fetched, alien concept to have multinational corporate companies competing against one another on our hallowed turf. However, what people define as "normal" shifts incrementally over time and eventually a new normal presents itself, one that is far different from its predecessor. Currently, there is resistance to Red Bull's invasion of football, particularly in German fandom — these hostile reactions are natural when the process initially advances itself. However, it eventually becomes normalised, as fandom (and wider society) begins to accept a new reality.

Supporters have an innate desire to watch elite footballers perform on the biggest stage. On the surface, there is nothing inherently wrong with this. However, the repetition of special events simply turns them into mediocre ones. Over time, they lose their spectacle, intrigue, drama, and then, eventually, their meaning. Every new milestone reached in this monopolisation process will always be presented as "progress" by the game's leading authorities, regardless of its core motivations. But whatever the future may hold, one thing is certain: as the rise of the monopolies continues, they're pulling the ladder up behind them.

Commercialisation

*Advertising may be described as the science of arresting human
intelligence long enough to get money from it.*
Stephen Leacock, Garden of Folly

It seems like every major competition in world football is being
scaled up, from the FIFA World Cup to the UEFA Champions
League. Why are football's governing bodies hellbent on
negotiating terms for larger-format tournaments? The answer
has everything to do with profit: more fixtures provide more
advertising opportunities.

In the twenty-first century, it's become impossible to watch
a televised game without seeing a constant barrage of corporate
sponsorship. We may think we're watching football, but that's
not how the advertisers see it. Like a combative midfielder,
the ads never stop running. Rampant commercialism is an
unfortunate by-product of neoliberalism's economic doctrine,
and it's not exclusive to football. Today, Western society
is awash with adverts, a rising tide which shows no sign of
abating. In 2007, marketing firm Yankelovich ran a survey
and discovered that the average person sees up to 5,000 ads
a day.[1] More recent research, undertaken by Forbes, estimates
that modern consumers are now exposed to approximately
10,000 ads a day.[2] For the figure to have doubled in such a
short timeframe is staggering, and proof that advertising is
infiltrating our daily lives more and more.

In a frenzy of corporate branding, it appears our clubs are on a mission to advertise as many products to us as they possibly can. But should we not be asking why this is being allowed to happen? True, sponsorship deals have created extra revenue streams for clubs, but at what cost to the integrity of our game? And how do these highly profitable advertising campaigns affect the general well-being not just of football supporters, but of wider society as a whole?

Companies spend huge amounts of money working out how best to hijack our attention. One of the main aims of the advertising sector is to instil a sense of want into the consumer by subconsciously inducing feelings of inadequacy. Then they present the perfect solution: their product. To compound the misery, advertising techniques are growing more sophisticated in their capacity to manipulate potential customers. Neuromarketing tactics have evolved to leverage certain psychological triggers such as FOMO (fear of missing out) and high-pressure strategies are employed to covertly stimulate anxiety. For the atomised consumer, retail therapy may feel like an effective coping mechanism in the short term, but these intense corporate marketing strategies are creating, and sustaining, the very environment which is responsible for inducing anxiety in the first place. It's a vicious cycle. Fakery and feigned enthusiasm have become the new normal — and we're all expected to play along. Previous generations would be struck by the sheer intensity of modern marketing strategies if they were to live a day in our shoes.

Today, football shirts are more like business advertisements than playing uniforms. By default, we've become walking corporate billboards and even pay shedloads of money for the privilege of wearing the garment. Without doubt, football clubs are culturally significant enough to exist as independent and sovereign entities. So how have we come to accept this? The beautiful game is being overwhelmed by an endless barrage of corporate advertising. Have we stopped caring? Or have we just given up questioning such logic?

It's rather easy, in a world of excessive consumerism, to forget that for more than a century, football's authorities had no interest in facilitating the presence of advertising companies. Moreover, its introduction to the sport was largely met, at least among fan communities, with derision and displeasure. Many initially rejected the notion, understanding that football's principles could easily be undermined by the arrival of advertisers. Reflecting upon the journey of this ever-increasing commercial cloud may allow us to grasp the real depths of its intrusion.

A Short History of Advertising in English Football

In 1970, the little remembered Watney Mann Invitation Cup — named after its sponsor, the Watney Mann brewery — presided over its inaugural season. Within three years, it had been unceremoniously canned. This rather unsuccessful tournament didn't resonate with fans in the way its sponsors had hoped or intended. Nevertheless, it left a defining legacy — advertising had entered football. Although it did not pre-empt an opening of the advertisement floodgates immediately, the seed had been planted.

Sponsoring cup competitions is one thing, but emblazoning a company name across a club's shirt is something else entirely. So which club was the original outlier? Which footballing institution was the first to degrade itself in the name of profit maximisation? Well, it was Kettering Town (yes, you did read that correctly).

In 1976, Kettering Town's board of directors had a cunning plan to make a fast buck, and Kettering Tyres were the first company to be branded across a competitive side's football shirt. However, this partnership was short-lived, as the FA promptly insisted on the removal of the graphic, citing a sponsorship ban that had been instituted only four years earlier in 1972 (it appears the FA used to take their own regulation seriously). Despite this setback, the plucky board members of Kettering Town were not to be stopped. By the summer of 1977, in collaboration with Derby County and Bolton Wanderers, their efforts were successful in lobbying the FA to overturn the sponsorship ban. Times were changing, the Overton Window was shifting, and an emboldened business class was now closing in on football. As neoliberal modes of thinking began to impact those who governed our game, sponsorship money was given rite of passage, thus helping pave the way for an economic and political revolution of the game.

Initially, as broadcasting regulations officially prevented advertising messages from being broadcast, branding was relatively limited. In 1981, the BBC even issued a small fine to a club for showing advertising during a televised game, suggesting there was still some resistance to this sponsorship invasion. However, such punishments were rare, and the old ideology simply couldn't hold out. With neoliberalism imposing itself on a wider scale, the BBC (just like the FA) became lax in the enforcement of its own longstanding codes of practice.

The 1982 League Cup became the first major competition to receive sponsorship. The National Dairy Council handed over £2 million to acquire naming rights for England's secondary domestic trophy, and subsequently re-branded it

"The Milk Cup". Moreover, with ever-increasing wage bills to pay and a competitive edge to uphold, football clubs could not afford to miss out on this new revenue stream. By 1987, within five years of the National Dairy Council's landmark move, every top-flight team had a sponsor emblazoned across their shirts. The introduction of weekly televised live football in 1983 had also provided a massive incentive to advertisers who could now display their brands to millions of eager viewers. Therefore, advances in broadcasting technology, coupled with a wider acceptance of neoliberal sensibilities, created the ideal conditions for a cultural shift in the footballing world towards commercialism.

The Advertising Explosion

With the stripping away of Rule 34's century-old protective legislation, football was hijacked by big business, as our national game became tethered to the pursuit of profit maximisation. Since then, the influence of sponsors has expanded year-on-year. The following decade saw Littlewoods secure sponsorship rights for the FA Cup, whilst Barclays claimed the newly constructed Premier League. If regulation is not put in place to temper it, then advertising will only continue to invade the game, with the industry finding new and innovative ways to showcase products. Advertising boards, once consisting of a basic logo or image, now dominate pitch side parameters, operating with astonishing brightness as pioneering optical illusions grab our attention. During the 2022 World Cup, pop-up scorelines accompanied by advertising slogans appeared on our screens, despite the scoreline being continuously displayed very clearly in the top-left corner. And who could forget Cristiano Ronaldo's request for "*agua*" at a press conference as he gazed at several Coca-Cola bottles strategically placed in front of him? This shows us that the advertising industry is no longer content with displaying propaganda in the background of media interviews, it's now setting up camp in the foreground as well. Empty screen space is a marketing *faux pas*, a missed opportunity to promote products and brainwash viewers.

The commercial fog engulfing our game continues to thicken. During the 2021/22 season, eight of the 20 Premier League clubs were sponsored by gambling firms, although not all these companies were British-based. English football's lax regulation opened a backdoor to foreign betting companies seeking to advertise their products to punters in countries where online gambling is illegal (such as China). To gain legal access to Premier League football kits, a foreign betting firm simply needs to set up in a UK-based offshore tax haven (and there are plenty to choose from). The gambling industry has been using English football as a vehicle to facilitate illegal wagering abroad, whilst our governing bodies conveniently turn a blind eye.

If there were any doubt as to the extent to which advertising is now controlling, influencing and restructuring football in its own image, then consider our stadiums. To help fund expansion and increase profit margins, clubs now apply commercial strategies that merge them with major sponsors. Our football grounds are being named after corporations, and equally alarming is how normal it all feels. Football grounds used to be named in relation to their geographical location, a traditional and logical custom. Today, they're being named after foreign airline companies and betting firms.

In what has now become "corporate football", everything has a sponsor. And shamefully, UEFA delegates routinely award themselves and their corporate sponsors with the largest percentage of cup final tickets. In 2022, the Stade de

France hosted the Champions League final. The two finalists (Liverpool and Real Madrid) received only 20,000 tickets each, whilst 23,000 tickets were gifted to UEFA and their affiliated partners. As a result of such policies, supporters are tempted into black markets and pay extortionate prices.

The arrogance and entitlement of the governing bodies, and the disdain shown to ordinary football fans, is dismantling the spirit traditionally associated with showpiece finals. Corporate businessmen are replacing loyal, passionate and deserving fans. Furthermore, this trend can also be seen inside the stadiums of Premier League clubs, sanitising the once vibrant atmospheres associated with England's top division. Today, an increasing amount of space is allocated to corporations and their partners at club grounds. Corporate boxes, more profitable but less soulful than the environment that surrounds them, are eating into standard viewing areas. In this commercial landscape, clubs prioritise wealthier "customers". As a result, many "legacy fans" have been priced out of their local stadium and replaced by tourists or the business class. But tourists are supposed to observe the atmosphere, not define it.

And it's not just our clubs that are subservient to the demands of corporate sponsors. Advertisers also control fixture lists, as consolidated stretches of televised football provide ample opportunity for consumer bombardment. Every season, managers and coaching staff rightfully protest about the huge number of games their teams play in a short space of time, particularly around the Christmas period. Injury lists grow and player's bodies struggle to cope, but their health is of no concern; branding into eyeballs is all that matters. Furthermore, kick-off times are held hostage to broadcasting requirements, which in turn prioritise consumer traffic times over common sense. Throughout the season, the self-regulated Premier League regularly flouts its own rules with regards to fixture dates being switched at the last minute. The result? Fans are unable to attend or left out of pocket as they desperately attempt to change travel plans. A hastily rearranged fixture can often mean that loyal supporters struggle to make the journey home due to insufficient public transport links, but, again, their trials and tribulations are of no concern.

Today, the entire football industry seems primarily focused on creating profit for vested interests as time and time again the wants of supporters are dismissed by football's governing authorities. Ironic slogans such as "football is for the fans" are broadcast to the masses in an attempt to further commercialise and commodify our love of the game. But we must also consider how this intrusive commercial cloud shapes our own attitudes and sensibilities. As the influence of the media sector continues to grow, its narrative increasingly impacts the way in which fans engage with football. In many respects, the advertising industry is playing a key role in turning football into a throwaway consumer entertainment package, devoid of any deeper meaning.

It's Not the Taking Part That Matters, It's the Winning That Counts

Another, cruder development has resulted from increasing advertisements, one that cuts at the very fabric of our sporting culture. This is the concept that victorious teams are the only ones who truly matter. Images of heroic champions holding their trophies aloft whilst basking in success are plastered everywhere — passionate, prestigious and perfect. Although such imagery could be deemed innocuous, with its continuous repetition younger football supporters might well ask: Why follow your "boring" local team when you could support the magnificent, all-conquering winning machine? The growth of the media and advertising industries has resulted in an increasing concentration of support for the large monopolies they showcase. Supporting a victorious club and cheering on the world's most exciting players is an easy way to feel part of something special — even if the connection is superficial. Buy the shirt and celebrate the victories because football is supposedly all about winning.

As a result of this, the local club loses its appeal. Individuals latch on to all-conquering clubs, favouring a distant corporation over standing on the terraces at their local ground. In this context, the perpetual promotion and glamorisation of winning by the media has served to drastically undermine localised networks and connections to smaller clubs. English fandom is gradually being ripped from its traditional roots and its unique identity diluted. As our clubs have treated us more and more like typical consumers, we have begun to behave as such, choosing to invest in winning teams in ever greater numbers. As local pride is buried and forgotten, another chunk of the people's game is hacked away.

Another by-product of this process is the escalating intolerance of losing. For some supporters of elite teams, losing doesn't even bear contemplating because football is a consumer product in which victory should be a prepaid guarantee. Football players posting on social media after a poor performance receive an onslaught of abuse, with defeat now inexcusable. However, if you follow a team purely because they win, you will always feel cheated by defeat, like it's not your club anymore. But this notion that "you must win" doesn't really make sense in the bigger picture. Throughout the pyramid, less than 5% of teams can win silverware in any given year. So what about the vast majority who don't? If winning is so critical, and 95% of teams don't win trophies, then why do we bother supporting our clubs at all? Clearly there are other factors driving our support. A meaningful and loyal connection to your local club is the most powerful force in fandom, however this is what the advertising industry undermines with its constant need to associate products with winners.

In order to temper this commercialisation, regulatory action is needed. For instance, if we were to reactivate the previous legislation and ban shirt sponsorship, then it would immediately begin to level the financial playing field and give clubs their identity back. Otherwise, if the current trend continues, then we must ask ourselves, how long it will be before companies such as Red Bull begin to rename English clubs? Would the promise of untold riches being pumped into your club persuade you that sponsorship is the only route to on-field success? Would you accept Red Bull (or for that matter any business brand) as part of your historic club's name? Whatever the answer, it's worth noting that perspectives shift over time — we used to think shirt sponsorship was excessive, but now we see it as a common-sense practice.

In modern sport, advertising not only sells products, but also sells *itself.* Posturing as a divine and patriarchal provider of all things, it engineers a psychological trap. We've been wrongly convinced that corporate branding is a natural part of the footballing landscape. But as advertising's domineering influence upon our national sport continues to grow, a pertinent truth is revealed: there was a reason why it was previously banned.

Privatisation

Whenever conflict arises among living creatures, the sense of ownership is the cause.

Shantideva

There are myriad ways to govern the football industry. Choosing the best way is a matter for politics, but there are a number of key issues to consider, chief amongst them the question of club ownership. Should clubs be owned privately or collectively? Or perhaps a combination of both? What about regulation? Which type? And how much or how little should be applied? The answers to these questions then impact how these institutions are to be managed — autocratically or democratically?

In England, current legislation allows football clubs to be privately owned by virtually anyone who is wealthy enough to afford them (the "fit and proper persons test" seems incredibly difficult to fail). But this ownership structure is not a natural consequence or a God-given right — it's a political decision, and one which has had huge ramifications for English fandom. Moreover, in light of recent developments, it's fair to suggest that this political decision warrants increased scrutiny.

In bygone eras, stakeholders were local businessmen and traditional supporters of the club they invested in. However, the landscape has changed significantly. Today, the owners of our biggest clubs are primarily overseas investors, and as a result the Premier League has morphed into a geopolitical playground. The ruling class of oil-rich foreign states have seized upon an opportunity afforded to them by English football's lack of protective regulation. With hundreds of billions of dollars idly floating in their investment funds, the goal of traditional profit maximisation may no longer even be a central aim. Instead, the soft power garnered through the ownership of a globally revered football club serves to sportswash state reputations. A handy enterprise if you're a dictatorship keen on consolidating power and improving your international reputation.

Moreover, an influx of US-based owners has descended upon the Premier League in recent times, as they seek to engage new markets amid a flurry of commercialisation. Revered sporting institutions in the US are comparatively expensive, but Premier League outfits can be acquired for a fraction of the price. Essentially, English football clubs have been left exposed to the pressures of a worldwide marketplace, and as a result they're being bought on the cheap by wealthy foreign investors.

Although a football club may struggle to balance its own books, it can still be beneficial to its proprietor in other ways. The glamour and prestige of owning a much-loved English football team can aid commercial strategies and business interests elsewhere. There are multiple reasons why someone might want to privately own a football club, and some of these will naturally conflict with the interests of local supporters. Indeed, the motivations of owners are becoming increasingly complex, but one thing is clear: the current ownership model for big English football clubs grants exclusive access to the financial elite. As it stands, a Premier League fanbase could never dream of owning their club. However, other countries have different ideas about how to govern the football industry, and offer alternatives to privatised, authoritarian-based systems.

The German Case Study

In Germany, the ownership model is defined by a rule known as "50+1", a crucial piece of legislation that upholds historical roots and encourages localised democratic procedure. This rule was introduced in 1998 when the German Football League (DFL) decided to amend its regulations, allowing clubs to operate as limited companies and thereby opening the door to private investment. The 50+1 rule ensures that club members retain majority control, with at least 50% plus one vote, thus blocking external investors from taking over the majority stake in a football club. In essence, 50+1 acts as a safeguarding measure, preventing wealthy individuals or corporate entities from controlling bigger clubs and using them as private commercial enterprises. As a result, German clubs are democratically run, with members (or supporters) enjoying a majority of the voting rights — at least 51%. Alternatively, in England, our governing bodies decided to forget that our safeguarding measure (Rule 34) ever existed.

German football opened its door to private and corporate finance around 15 years later than English football, albeit with a critical caveat in place: German clubs are still the property of their respective supporters — just. For obvious reasons, this democratic ownership model is off-putting to potential private investors, as, due to the weighting of its governance structure, these profiteers can be outvoted by fans.

There are critics of the German 50+1 rule, and there are also loopholes around its protective regulation (RB Leipzig being the most obvious example). However, supporter groups fight fiercely for its continuation. In light of recent threats to this system from predatory financial elites, a new fan-led campaign has emerged in Germany entitled "50+1 stays!". Even though fans are aware that the model obstructs large investments flooding into clubs, they're keen to stick by it. Some dissenting voices can be heard, frustrated about the lack of opportunity for private investment, however the overriding majority of Germans are willing to sacrifice monetary gains for democratic control. This example of defiant solidarity should resonate with English fandom. When comparing us to our German counterparts, it's difficult not to wonder why we haven't engaged in any such meaningful acts of resistance.

The 50+1 rule has protected Bundesliga clubs from the over-commercialisation that has tarnished the English game. The effects of this improved ownership model can be seen and heard on the terraces. German fandom is characterised by high levels of engagement, deep passion and a strong representation of the social connections that a football club should engender. With members playing a direct role in influencing how clubs are managed, there is a more profound impact on local communities, and fans enjoy greater liberties. The commitment to keeping matchday and season ticket prices low ensures that individuals from less affluent backgrounds can still attend games, enhancing accessibility for a broader spectrum of supporters. In 2023/24, the average (standing) season ticket price in the Bundesliga was €205 Euros (£175). If you're comparing this figure to English top-tier season ticket prices (which don't include the option of standing because we are not allowed to do that), then I formally apologise for adding that every season ticket sold in Germany includes free public transport to the ground.[1] Moreover, Germany's fan-friendly approach extends to offering concessions of up to 50%

for children, the elderly and disabled supporters. In contrast to practices in England, alcoholic beverages are sold cheaply inside stadiums and members are permitted to drink them in their seats. For the many fans who don't wish to sit down, safe standing areas are allocated in every ground. Such liberties are in stark contrast to the conditions suffered by English fandom.

More than mere consumers, supporters' groups regularly use their clubs as a platform to celebrate causes or highlight social concerns, often displaying large banners before and during games. They take strong political stances on issues such as racism, sexism and homophobia within the framework of their football community. This engagement highlights the integral role football clubs can play in advocating for positive social change — German fans use their clubs as a vehicle through which to empower themselves. There is no distance between supporter and club, because the two are merged into one entity.

This collectivised ownership model certainly seems to generate a more meaningful connection between supporter and club. For instance, when Union Berlin was in financial trouble, thousands of fans took advantage of a government scheme which paid citizens for donating blood. Huge amounts of funds were raised by Union Berlin supporters literally bleeding for their club (this incredible fanbase also collectively rebuilt their own crumbling and neglected stadium, donating their time and effort for free). But there is another element supported by this dynamic: self-esteem. Unlike English fans, football fans in Germany have the belief that they can affect change and the political will to collectively organise and fight for justice. The "50+1 stays!" movement is not a standalone example. "*Unsere Kurve*" is a coalition of supporters' groups from across Germany whose main priority is to protect fan interests and counter the relentless tide of commercialisation which has swept over the modern game. For example, when broadcasters introduced Monday night football into the Bundesliga calendar, German fandom reacted angrily at the disdain shown to supporters who may be unable to attend far-away fixtures due to work commitments. To oppose this development, meetings were held by fans and many public protests ensued, including supporters not entering the ground for the first 15 minutes of a game, displaying a televised empty stadium to the whole nation — an advertiser's nightmare. Eventually, after six hard-fought years, *Unsere Kurve* won the battle against the broadcasters and Monday night fixtures were abandoned by the DFL. In January 2024, *Unsere Kurve* struck again. From remote-controlled toy cars to planes mounted with smoke bombs, German supporters launched a series of sustained (and very creative) protests aimed at disrupting Bundesliga fixtures. The aim was to prevent the DFL from selling its media rights to a private equity firm. At an estimated £850 million, this was no small deal. By February 2024, the DFL admitted defeat and the proposed media deal was called off. Once again, a nationwide coalition of German supporters' groups were victorious in the face of seemingly insurmountable odds. And here is a lesson for us: by uniting as a political force and coordinating protests, football fandom is capable of enacting meaningful change and defeating entrenched commercial interests.

Compared to the riches pouring into the English Premier League, German football clubs are at a financial disadvantage, but German fans understand what would be sacrificed should they leave the door ajar to majority privatised ownership. The unfreedoms imposed on fandom by neoliberalism's commercialisation agenda are clearly apparent in other footballing nations. Evidently, they've decided it isn't worth it. As English football paves the way for continued billionaire investment, these acts of resistance must be applauded.

Back to Our Reality

In England, our clubs are governed autocratically *for* us, not democratically *with* us. This dynamic creates a constant conveyor belt of conflicts and tensions between supporter and owner, although it's obviously the latter in the driving seat. Ultimately, it's club owners who can effortlessly assert their dominance over fanbases, given that property assets — in this context *their* football club — are preserved and guaranteed through UK law. Therefore, our system itself is a mechanism for shielding club owners, leaving them invulnerable to attack.

In England, despite often being ironically informed that "football is for the fans", supporters are consciously aware that they hold no hard power. However, club owners do sometimes afford fan bodies a certain amount of illusory soft power, which allows them to influence club affairs (but only to a limited extent, of course). After all, it's in the interest of club owners to keep fans onside wherever possible. In short, sometimes club owners pretend to listen to fans.

An example of this soft power in action could be seen relatively recently at my local club, Leeds United. In 2018, the boardroom leadership team decided to change the design of the club crest. The new concept presented a cartoon torso conducting "the Leeds salute", a passionate call to arms regularly seen on the terraces of Elland Road. It proved to be extremely unpopular. As a result of an online backlash from fans, the club wisely listened to the feedback and withdrew their plans — the soft power of the collective fanbase was victorious.

However, the parameters of what this soft power can achieve are set in the boardroom. When push comes to shove, English club infrastructures are top-down dictatorships whose interests are exclusively controlled by the will of its shareholders (often foreign-based investors with no allegiance to local interests). If one ignores a club's PR machine and considers the economic decisions made in isolation, then the true intentions of an owner become clearer.

In 2021, Leeds United fans were officially encouraged to purchase a new crypto currency, after it emerged that Chiliz, a leading crypto firm focused on sports and entertainment-based entities, had partnered with the club. The promotion of crypto currencies has become increasingly common for Premier League teams, and the intention is obvious: to manipulate the fans in order to extract profit for partners. Ultimately, cryptocurrencies lend themselves to gambling, which all Premier League clubs have shown themselves to be happy to promote.

Many Leeds supporters were outraged at this blatant money-making scam and identified the tangible risks involved. Did the club relent and apologise? No. This time, profit margins were directly involved, and, inevitably, the club stood firm. Therefore, despite fan resistance, the Chiliz brand was officially endorsed by the club. Here lies one of the key driving forces in our supporter-owner relationship: when profit can be made, the illusion of "togetherness" is shattered, the moral compass is dropped and the total authority of the dictator is exercised.

The contradiction between the cold-hearted, ruthless business side of club operations, and the warm-hearted and caring nature of organised fan groups is stark. In every fanbase throughout the country, passionate volunteers exist, setting up food banks or organising charitable donations. Our clubs' trust organisations are made up of dedicated fans all focused upon doing good deeds in the name of their club, sacrificing large chunks of their time to help those in need without receiving any financial compensation, whereas those in charge of our clubs advertise multiple betting companies and poorly regulated cryptocurrencies to their own fans. We see it time and time again from club owners throughout England: profit before people, the reverse of how a football club should be run.

Democratic Models

In March 2020, during the UK's initial Covid-19 lockdown, I began to interview people for a podcast series dedicated to Marcelo Bielsa called *The Bielsa Bible*. Coordinating correspondence via Zoom calls and lengthy e-mail exchanges, I began to build relationships with residents of his homeland, Argentina. The individuals interviewed were deeply engaged with the footballing world. Interestingly, they all expressed an opinion on how English football clubs were run, quickly determining it to be "strange" in nature. To their mind, the idea of a football club being privately owned is an alien concept.

As part of the podcast series, I interviewed Patricio Miller, a typical Argentinian football fan. In perfect English, he stated:

The first thing I would do is point out a subtlety: if a club does not belong to its "*socios*"/members, I would not call it a club; I would call it a company. I am not saying that Leeds United does not belong spiritually to the people, but materially it belongs to the owner(s). The democratic club is the correct path, the one that adjusts to the interests and purposes of a club. If something does not go well, then it will have to be corrected within those parameters, not outside of them. The culture of sporting and economic success perverts everything. I want a club close to home and close to the community. I want a club to send my children to play sports (and not just football!), so that they can make friends. A club that encourages the people from the city or town go to the football game on Sunday with family or friends, to spend a few hours at the club headquarters on a Thursday afternoon, and meet the schoolteacher, the bricklayer and the bus driver. I want a club that organises events and raises money when a neighbour's house is flooded, a club that solves the problem of a homeless citizen and applauds the scientist who has won an international award in biology. I want a club to feel part of something, to promote and stimulate an identity. And I don't want an entrepreneur's money to debase any of those things.

To Patricio, a club is more than a football team. Matters away from the pitch count just as much as those on it. In England, we only entertain half of the narrative. However, Patricio does concede some present disadvantages within the Argentinian democratic system. Financial mismanagement and nepotism certainly still occur, and short-term strategies used in an attempt to make leaders more popular with voters (members) often prevail. True, Patricio acknowledges that it's not a perfect system. However, he would never allow his club to be transformed into a company, owned by a businessman and used as private property. No amount of money pumped in by an outside party would change that. Patricio has the same attitude as the passionate German fan groups discussed earlier. Every system has its flaws, and the implementation of a collectively owned democratic system would not be without bumps in the road. However, those who have adopted this style of governance are fighting tooth and nail to keep it. What does this tell us?

Remarkably, here in the UK there are also green shoots of democratic growth. The fans of Scottish Premier League club Heart of Midlothian were pushed to the brink, and so decided to formulate a plan and fight back. The club is now completely fan-owned. In order to fully understand how this came to pass, I liaised with sports reporter and STV presenter Jamie Borthwick, an expert on Scottish football.

The Hearts' story is a classic example of the problems and possibilities that define modern football — one of financial mismanagement, global capital and a stubborn, committed cadre of local fans. Come 2004, Chris Robinson, Hearts' owner, had plunged the club into nearly £20 million of debt. To try and make amends, he concocted a cunning scheme. His intention was to sell Tynecastle Park, where the club had been based for more than 100 years and move to a groundshare with Scottish rugby at Murrayfield. The supporters were less than happy to say the least, and the campaign group "Save Our Hearts" was formed. The group successfully stopped the sale and forced Robinson out of the club. It was then bought by Lithuanian entrepreneur Vladimir Romanov in 2005, who spent tens of millions of pounds on players and went through any number of managers. Over time, Romanov seemed to lose interest in the club, and, amid speculation that his bank in the Baltic nation was in trouble, Hearts entered administration in 2013.

The Save Our Hearts group now found itself called upon to rescue the club once again, this time reforming as Foundation of Hearts. This small cadre of supporters had been laying the groundwork for a fan-led takeover for a number of years and when the opportunity came, they were ready to step up. Having seen fans rally to buy (worthless) shares for hundreds of pounds just to keep the club going, they reasoned that there might be sufficient enthusiasm to raise enough cash to buy the club. The legal issues around the club's administration meant they needed a couple of million pounds up front, and so they quietly approached Ann Budge, a millionaire IT entrepreneur and season ticket holder in Tynecastle's Wheatfield Stand. It was agreed that if she would put up the £2.3 million required to save Hearts, then the fans would pay her back and then take control. Due to Romanov's waning interest, the club's crumbling infrastructure was in urgent need of repair. It was decided that the 8,000 supporters who were already pledging £10 a month would first finance the rebuilding of the club and then pay back Budge. That plan took slightly longer, but Budge had been paid back in full by the end of 2020. The club waited until the Coronavirus restrictions ended before allowing fans back in the stadium and then announced a full handover of shares to the fans in August 2021.

Here, a small, dedicated and forward-thinking group of local supporters managed to take democratic control of their football club — via the help of a wealthy individual who was happy to play the role of temporary custodian. This event should provide a possible blueprint for clubs in England and beyond. If a club is unfortunately placed into administration, then there is an opportunity for a movement of fans to collectively raise funds and agree a CVA with administrators. Granted, there needs to be an element of organisation within the ranks, and you may need to find a local Ann Budge who can help stump up the cash, but evidently it can be done. A network of fans sought to liberate Hearts and have achieved full ownership of their club. Board members are accountable to all fans who contribute a small monthly donation to infrastructure costs but are still empowered to manage the day-to-day running of the club. Fans have the power to utilise a statutory mechanism to vote in new proposals or vote out boardroom representatives.

Moreover, the Hearts fanbase can now influence the culture and ethics of their club, and even decide how and where bigger investments should be made. They have gained control. The Hearts Foundation decided to lay down the law with a few totems, establishing certain things that the club will never be able to do without the express permission of fans — a set of simple, but very important rules that are central to protecting the club's unique identity: Tynecastle will always be their home, their iconic maroon and white colours will remain intact, and their club's name must be preserved. These demands are non-negotiable, with fans exercising a degree of hard power on those trusted to oversee club operations. This does not mean that supporters turn up at the ground on a Monday morning, modelling a suit and tie, whilst digging through commercial finances. On the contrary, they employ competent professionals to do it for them. The fans' mantra has always been that Hearts will be "fan-owned, not fan-run", and this is a concept that should be adopted by football clubs south of the border.

Fan ownership is a fast-growing concept in Scotland, and to date it has been achieved at a number of Scottish Premier League clubs including: Hearts, Motherwell and St Mirren. Interestingly, and rather encouragingly, this movement is also beginning to take root in English football. Although every team in the upper echelons of our pyramid system remains in private hands, there are now over 50 fan-owned clubs in the English pyramid competing in the lower tiers, including Exeter City and AFC Wimbledon. Fan ownership may be a relatively new phenomenon, but its roots are deepening as the draw of self-determination and true independence becomes increasingly appealing.

Many fan-owned clubs have been set up in a proactive manner, with supporters creating a football club that genuinely represents them and their interests. However, collective ownership has also been established in a reactive way, often due to a debt crisis, as the private model fails a club financially. Sometimes supporters have no choice, it's either take ownership into their own hands or watch their beloved club die. When a club's finances have been wrecked by incompetent or reckless individuals, the private sector is often conspicuous by its absence, with would-be investors put off by a mountain of liabilities. But supporters of a debt-ridden club have no such inhibitions — to them it's not an investment opportunity, it's their church, and it must be saved.

In 2013, Portsmouth FC were in dire straits and ridden with debt after successive relegations and administrations. Liquidation was looming. In April of that year, the Portsmouth Supporters Trust (PST) officially took over ownership of the club. After just 18 months in charge, the Trust's 2,300 dedicated members had paid back creditors and the club was declared debt-free. There are numerous examples of the private ownership model's failure to govern, with individuals effectively sinking a football club and then jumping ship, but not so with collective models of ownership. In fact, the recent case studies of Portsmouth FC and Hearts show us that fan-ownership produces quite the opposite effect — with all hands on deck, supporters rally and repair the ship at any cost.

Despite their successful intervention, Portsmouth FC supporters then decided to sell their club back into private hands. Indeed, the idea that football clubs should be privately owned is still ingrained within England's footballing culture. But it's important to note that today's model of privatisation is far removed from earlier eras of English football. Previously, clubs operated with local businessmen at the helm and were protected by much tighter regulatory controls. This fine balance ensured that English football clubs were generally run in the interests of supporters — an effective ownership model that spanned generations. However, with the abandonment of Rule 34 and the impact of unfettered globalisation, our clubs are no longer community-facing institutions.

In the wake of all the greed, self-interest and outright contempt being shown towards loyal supporters (from governing bodies as well as clubs), English fandom must surely begin to debate alternative models of ownership. The goalposts have long since shifted, and today's model of privatisation is trashing the past and wrecking the present. If serfdom is our lot, then surely it's time we looked towards the future and started to think differently.

Part 2

Gaining Control

A New Ideology

The measure of intelligence is the ability to change.
                                                        Albert Einstein

English football is beset with many problems. Supporters are overlooked and exploited; a process of over-commercialisation is damaging the integrity of the game; fair competition is forever diminishing; and the entire economic system is laden with debt. Undoubtably, the community aspect of our national game is being undermined. For want of a better phrase, football seems to be "losing its soul".

None of these outcomes, however, are natural or inevitable; they're manmade. As billionaires and millionaires enrich themselves via a system of their own design, the rest of us pay the price. And herein lies a main concern: we complain about "the state of the game" whilst uncritically absorbing the economic philosophy responsible for creating these conditions in the first place. The neoliberal formula always creates the same outcomes: huge debt burdens, a process of deregulation and large-scale privatisation. Consequently, as markets are opened up to international investors, national and regional sovereignty become subordinate to the wants of overseas stakeholders. It's a political framework which has destroyed what used to be referred to as "the people's game". In order to resolve the issues listed above, which are symptoms of a wider systemic failure, the football industry must be influenced by different intellectual foundations — it needs a new ideology.

The following section theorises a transference of power away from unelected financial elites and over to ordinary people in a political model which prioritises collectivism. For those who may have reservations about implementing such a policy in wider society, a compromise is offered. By focusing on a tiny segment of the UK's national economy, a controlled experiment could be undertaken. What would happen if all neoliberal economic practice was reverse-engineered? The premise is simple, the outcomes produced by deregulated marketisation could be bettered through a process of heavy state investment, long-term strategic thinking, effective regulation and a well-planned economy. Our entire domestic football industry could be ringfenced by government, thus offering the perfect platform to test such a theory.

An alternative political framework for the governance of English football is proposed, one that has democracy at its core and actively seeks a more even distribution of wealth. A progressive and forward-thinking, state-led initiative which opens the door to regional independence, financial transparency and economic security. A totally new outlook promoting equality, sporting integrity and at its heart an ideology that seeks to transform English fandom into a more engaged, partisan and politically active entity.

Before examining this potential transition in any detail, we must first take a step back and debunk a piece of inherited "logic" which underpins the current framework. And, like all great myths, it's based on a half-truth. This is the notion that football is a business. It's a very important categorisation because, to any rational mind, if football *is* a business, then, by default, we represent a marketplace of consumers. Is that *really* how you relate to your club? Perish the thought — you're not a consumer, but a passionate supporter, and you've no doubt got the emotional scars to prove it. Fandom's relationship to football clubs adds a layer of uncomfortable complexity that the word *business* cannot possibly represent because it excludes the spiritual and social elements that make football into something more than just a game.

Let's Not Get Down to Business

Football started flirting with the business realm during the Victorian era, when clubs began to operate as limited companies, undertaking infrastructure development projects and paying the wages of professional players. However, the Victorians wisely aimed to preserve football's foundational truths, and henceforth governed the game in a way that ensured sporting integrity would be upheld. To restrict private profiteers and promote community relations, they created Rule 34. Furthermore, fair competition was ensured via the sharing of gate receipts and the implementation of a salary cap. The Victorian message resonates loud and clear: football is first and foremost a sport, and its business element is to be strictly regulated.

When a business is under private ownership, it's under no obligation to appease the wider community. What makes the commerce of football so unusual is that football clubs have people who support them unconditionally. That is not how the world of business typically operates. In a competitive marketplace, when business output is poor, consumers will likely buy from a direct competitor. The system is about brand loyalty, not blind loyalty. Football clubs, however, have "customers" who will buy into their product regardless of how well it performs — this reality betrays market sensibilities.

Put simply, football is at odds with the business world, and therefore, ultimately, it doesn't strictly belong there.

Our football clubs are community assets, and Rule 34 suggested this concept extremely clearly. It's also important to stress that most businesses will fail eventually, and this should never be the fate of any passionately supported football club. The 2021 *Crouch Report* sheds light on this issue. Author and journalist Ian King summarises:

> In amongst all the recommendations made by the government's fan-led review into the governance of football, there is one common thread. Football is more than a business. It occupies a unique place at the heart of our culture and has a value which can't be easily measured.[1]

To feel a deep sense of belonging and be part of something bigger than your own inner subjective thoughts and feelings is a rare and elusive concept. Within modern football, these emotions are currently being monetised in pursuit of corporate profits. Strange and alien language has even defined us as "legacy fans" who are to be overlooked in the pursuit of outward commercial expansion. Instead, such emotional bonds should be celebrated and central to a club's core objectives. With regards to strategy discussion, a football club's leading hierarchy should ask: how do we enrich the local community we are here to serve? How do we repay their loyalty and create a Blitz spirit of us against the world? If a football club built an economic model around such an approach, it would benefit supporters, the club itself and the region as a whole.

Clearly, to many of us, football is more than just another pastime, it actually defines our identity. For some, it's a quasi-religious faith, fostering deeply spiritual and emotional bonds between supporters and clubs which are sustained through generations. To classify our football clubs as "typical businesses", surviving in a dog-eat-dog world, is to miss the point entirely. Should churches, mosques or synagogues be exposed to the cut-and-thrust of profit-maximisation and closed down if they fail? Obviously not, as they're recognised religious institutions giving meaning, hope and a sense of belonging to the lives of their followers. But for the millions of die-hard fans in this country, is a football club not providing a very similar service? That is not to suggest that football clubs should be reclassified as genuine religious institutions, rather to acknowledge that they exist somewhere in the in-between, as a hybrid entity. A football club is the round circle in the middle of a Venn diagram, overlapping sporting entertainment, social club, business operation and quasi-religious institution.

I would like to argue that a football club's main priority should be that of providing a service. A club represents a group of people with a shared interest; its primary functions include providing entertainment, enjoyment and societal bonding. An improved model could award football clubs an elevated status, above that of a typical business, one that recognises their importance in the hearts and minds of the people who follow them. In fact, if the entire football industry could be redefined as a service, then a brand new ideological framework through which to govern the game emerges. Such a reclassification would certainly suit us better — a business works for profit, whereas a service works for people.

Football is a communal and social pursuit; it belongs in the public sphere. Such a statement may raise eyebrows, but it also raises a number of questions, chief amongst the age-old issue of state intervention. Recently, privatisation has been winning the day in this ongoing ideological tug-of-war. However, the lack of democratic accountability and the turbulent economic environment in which football finds itself are clear signs that the current system is simply not fit for purpose. The same could be said, of course, about the wider world.

The Failure of Privatisation

Over the past few decades, the British state has ironically played an active role in diminishing its own power. Thatcherism, closely associated with the economic theories of Milton Friedman, triggered this political shift. The collapse of the Keynesian post-war economic consensus led to a growing conviction that government interference was generally a bad idea. As a result, we now live in a world completely dominated by the financial sector — it controls our politicians and undermines our democracy.

Yet while neoliberals often decry state intervention as unnecessary meddling, we have seen the state intervene on numerous occasions in order to save the very system which undermines it, particularly in the wake of the 2008 economic crash. In this circumstance, a lack of protective regulation allowed financial profiteers to gamble recklessly, knowing full well that the taxpayer would bail them out if necessary. The recent global pandemic has once again seen the state intervene, resulting in an orgy of corruption with government actors accused of funnelling millions into the bank accounts of personal associates via a litany of dodgy contracts. These examples (and many more) reveal a hypocritical nature to the neoliberal stance on state intervention: when it comes to saving reckless financial institutions or doling out taxpayers' money to cronies, state largesse is seemingly accepted as common sense, however providing free school meals to primary school children (at a fraction of the price) is considered controversial. In reality, whether a state *should* intervene in certain matters is not actually the issue at all because state intervention is always unavoidable. The debate is rather *to what degree*.[2] A laissez-faire approach to regulation is in itself decisive state intervention, so too is a shrinking of governmental responsibility.

Everywhere in the economy, from transport to utilities, the model of privatisation is falling under increased scrutiny. Thatcher may have claimed to stand for patriotism and national pride, but her economic rationale gifted British state assets directly into the hands of foreign firms whose goal is profiteering at our expense. The British now pay the highest train fares in Europe, despite a crumbling and neglected network. Unbelievably, privatised water companies are dumping raw sewage into our seas and rivers because they can't afford to dispose of it properly (despite having paid out billions to shareholders). Compounding the misery further, privatised gas and oil companies rake in huge profits from energy price hikes whilst people struggle to heat their homes. Busy food banks are a consistent component of contemporary life, and now even "warm banks" have been created, a brand-new development which offers further evidence of our county's economic and social decline. Families are deciding whether to "heat or eat" — a damning indictment of a system which fails to support everyday people. The NHS continues to be under-funded, with services increasingly fragmented and core employees grossly underpaid. The road to its ultimate destruction is well underway. As the institution decays, its hard-working staff remain overworked and undervalued. Clapping doesn't pay the bills.

Ultimately, this programme of mass privatisation has failed, and, once again, we have reached a turning point. As power dynamics continue to shift in favour of a tiny elite, we must re-calibrate ourselves to address and tackle the injustice of the current system. In our contemporary political landscape, perhaps the importance of the footballing realm has been grossly underestimated. With its huge cultural significance, its economic footprint across a variety of sectors and a hugely influential role in shaping public discourse, the football sector represents a key strategic battleground in a much wider political fight. If it could be taken, then the repercussions would be enormous. But the first port of call would be creating a better framework for our game, one that protects prosperity and integrity, rather than upholding greed and corruption. As the age of market fundamentalism reaches its limits, now is the perfect time to ringfence our national sport and trial a new economic philosophy.

Reverse-Engineering Neoliberalism

Why not redesign the system to serve the interests of the wider population? Football should be restructured with community, accessibility, democracy and traditional sporting integrity at the heart of its ideological framework. A model which sought to reverse-engineer neoliberal economic practice within the footballing sector could pursue the following policies:

- The widespread implementation of protective regulations.
- The eradication of debt.
- Collective ownership models.
- The installation of democratic procedures.

Over recent decades, the application of protective regulation has been more reactive than forward-thinking. Rules are complex and full of loopholes. Moreover, the current fiscal guidelines do more to protect the on-field dominance of the biggest clubs than anything else. A whole book could be dedicated to the financial mismanagement or financial misdemeanours of football clubs in the modern era. Nevertheless, it's important to understand that all these problems have systemic foundations. In order to prevent them from occurring in the first place, it would make sense to create a stricter and far more robust financial framework. Debt is not an inevitable consequence, it's a political choice and a form of control.

Today, a football club's first priority has to be profit margins (or, rather, debt management), because that is what the overarching ideological framework demands. It's certainly feasible, and one could argue practical, to remove such needless financial stress from the system altogether. The paranoia and uncertainty of business should not impact our clubs; administrations and liquidations belong in the commercial realm — football is a sport.

And how should sporting competitions be regulated? As we have seen, the distribution system employed by the Premier League is a meritocracy, financially rewarding those that perform well and offering far less compensation to those that don't. If you were to devise an economic programme which endeavoured to strengthen competition throughout the league, it would apply exactly the opposite principle. For instance, in American football's National Football League (NFL), the division's weakest teams are given first choice in selecting the best talent from the annual draft, in which emerging NFL players are selected by franchises. This approach is honoured to ensure that the league remains as competitive as possible. From 2003 to 2023, no less than 13 different teams won the Super Bowl (and at the time of writing, no franchise has ever claimed it for three consecutive seasons). When it comes to elite-level competitiveness, English football could perhaps learn a lesson from US sporting systems.

There is also a more nuanced argument for reversing the monopolisation process. People don't always find games particularly entertaining when negative tactics result in a lack of attacking play. Although such tactics are part and parcel of football, some of the reasons behind teams adopting them can be linked directly to its governance. The monopolisation process has resulted in wealthier clubs fielding far superior teams, and therefore attempting to "kill a game" by defending and slowing down the play is the only realistic option available to inferior opposition. Moreover, the financial consequences of relegation are now so severe that managers feel compelled to play "risk-averse" football in a desperate bid to avoid the drop. Therefore it could be argued that football's current system of governance is creating conditions which make negative styles of play more likely. Instead, authorities should find ways to promote more expansive styles of play because, on the whole, people find these more entertaining and by extension more enjoyable to watch.

A lack of protective regulation has also impacted English football off the pitch. During the 2023/24 season, 75% of Premier League clubs had majority owners from outside the UK. Is this what the majority of us want? Subjecting English football clubs to the advances of international investors has not been without controversy. Indeed, state intervention into English football has already happened. Oil-rich dictatorships are now controlling English football clubs, but with allegations of state-sanctioned murder, financial corruption and widespread concerns about human rights issues, English football's moral integrity is under the spotlight more than ever.

In a wider historical sense, many fanbases have felt frustrated by club owners who act with impunity and care not for the wants of supporters. Time and time again, the current system of authoritarianism produces terrible outcomes for loyal fans — when people's opinions are not heard, they feel disempowered, helpless and frustrated. Alternatively, the best way to prevent supporters from being overlooked or exploited is to give them a democratic say in how things are run. Football clubs should be institutions in which people feel empowered, important and respected. As Winston Churchill so famously alluded, democracy isn't a perfect system, but it's the best one we've got with regards to achieving those ends.

From the running of clubs to the governance of ruling authorities, English football should be fully democratised. This would ensure that decisions, both big and small, are made by a general consensus. Moreover, with moral integrity in mind, it would make sense to democratically decide upon a guiding set of principles for overall management. A written constitution could provide a framework for the long-term governance of the game and future-proof it from the meddling of political opportunists.

Along with the democratisation of our national sport should come a model of shared ownership. A football club is a community asset, so why shouldn't this be reflected in its ownership structure? Football and big business may be interlocked, but a process of privatisation is not a necessary by-product of this dynamic. There are different ways to manage this relationship. The beautiful game is a communal and social pursuit, so why can't football's business operations also be democratised and collectively owned?

There are facets of globalisation which could prove to be extremely advantageous. Because of its unrivalled worldwide popularity, English football has a huge gravitational pull, attracting a wide range of corporations into its orbit. Broadcasting services, gambling companies, garment manufacturers, drinks manufacturers, transport services, digital communications platforms and many other businesses all make huge annual profits in association with our national sport. Ultimately, English football is in big demand, and this provides us with an opportunity. An entrepreneurial British state could invest heavily in industries related to football, protect them from the advances of private shareholders and hand over collective ownership to us. By assuming full control of supply-side economics and delivering our product (English football) direct to the worldwide marketplace, a collectively owned manufacturing sector could eradicate billionaires completely from football's monetary system. Not only could this streamline the business model, but it would also free us from the authoritarianism of privatisation and reclaim our national sovereignty. Big business does not need to be seen as a necessary evil in relation to modern football, rather it presents a huge opportunity to trial a new form of collective ownership on an industrial scale.

The football industry also boosts other sectors such as construction and hospitality. Undoubtably, it plays a defining role in our national economy and democratising this process could reap huge societal benefits. Furthermore, from a cultural standpoint, our national game has a colossal impact on not only us, but also the wider world. Because of English football's worldwide popularity, the Premier League exerts huge amounts of soft power at a global level and this influence plays a prominent role in cultivating our country's reputation on the international stage. Do we really want this soft power to be weaponised by commercial interests or authoritarian-minded states? Should we not be using it to showcase and celebrate what our footballing heritage really means to us, our families and our communities? As previously noted, the neoliberal model is not particularly compatible with traditional sporting values, so perhaps it's time to try a new initiative. In an unstable and unpredictable wider economy, the footballing realm offers space for such political experimentation.

Collective Ownership of English Football

If football is to undergo a much-needed economic and social transformation, then a shift in the balance of power is required. The current model of privatisation must be swept aside and replaced by a radical, progressive agenda, one committed to democratic governance and collectivised ownership. Simply put, the *people* of the people's game need to be empowered by an economic model that serves society, not elites. However, such a logic has been notably absent in our contemporary political landscape. Indeed, a transition from private to public ownership would be bucking the trend of recent government policy.

The logic underpinning the process of denationalisation dictates that the private sector is more "efficient" in delivering outcomes as it's unburdened by government bureaucracy. However, throughout the UK's four-decade-long process of privatisation, a complete reversal of this "logic" has revealed itself. With regards to delivering public services, the attempts of some private contractors have been quite frankly laughable, with firms such as Carillion, G4S, Capita and Serco marred by scandals and plagued by a litany of failures. In reality, the so-called "efficiency" of the private sector often involves cutting costs through chronic underinvestment. All the while, wealthy elites enrich themselves further at the public's expense as services are consistently undermined. Just consider the current state of our utilities, health service or public transport systems. This financialised model of public procurement has proven to be wholly *inefficient* in serving the British public.

To further exacerbate the situation, government policies involving privatisation and financialisaton have substantially increased the UK's national debt burden. For example, future debt repayments tied to Public Finance Initiatives (a scheme initiated by Tony Blair's New Labour) are poised to shift over £199 billion from the public to the private sector.[1] However, a state can borrow money at a far cheaper rate than any private firm, so the creation of large-scale infrastructure projects is far more cost-effective within the public domain. Therefore, the "logic" underpinning the privatisation of the public sphere doesn't actually exist.

Policies involving reduced government spending epitomise the wider Thatcherite political agenda (the financial sector excluded). The conventional wisdom of neoliberal thought often declares that state investment counts as a financial liability on government balance sheets, a worrying debt burden which will rebound in the face of future generations. It's an economic ideology defined by short-term thinking. However, a good state investment can only be viewed as an asset, particularly if it serves the interests of the public and creates profits in the long-term. During a period of economic decline, when banks lose confidence in lending, business investment dries up and people have less disposable income, government expenditure can dig a country out of recession. There are numerous historical examples of this, for instance Clement Attlee's post-war economic strategy which tackled the UK's colossal debt burden by spending big on various public schemes, such as the NHS. In the wake of the Great Depression, US fiscal policy shifted towards conducting huge investment schemes in what became known as the New Deal. In both examples, national debt eventually reduced because these government-backed stimulus packages raised productivity and helped the economy grow in the long-term.

Savvy government investment schemes can also create entirely new sectors within the economy. Throughout the second half of the twentieth century, the US government (usually associated with a small-state mentality) often deviated away from the neoliberal agenda and injected huge amounts of patient capital into subsidising vast research and development (R&D) programs. As a result of these forward-thinking government initiatives, the US economy grew exponentially as it capitalised on a flurry of technological innovations. For example, the highly lucrative "tech boom" associated with California's Silicon Valley would not have been possible without heavy state investment into software R&D projects. Because shareholders are primarily focused on realising short-term financial gains, there are many market failures that the private sector simply can't fix without government support. Indeed, a booming national economy requires a well-balanced blend of state-backed and private initiatives (the "Japanese miracle" of the 1960s could not have happened without central government assuming an entrepreneurial role in business development schemes).

Running a national economy should not be confused with running a household or a typical business. A government is an organisation unlike any other, with its own bank, thus meaning it has no credit limit. Therefore, when UK politicians declare that they must implement austerity measures to stabilise the economy, they are of course being somewhat economical with the truth. Contrary to what previous Prime Minister Theresa May claimed, the "magic money tree" *does* exist, and it's called the Bank of England. Unfortunately, since the 2008 economic crash, its unprecedented quantitative easing measures have been targeted mainly towards bolstering a reckless financial sector. As a result, the real economy has suffered, productivity has declined, and national debt has increased.

But why repeat the mistakes of the past? Instead, borrowing should be used for the purpose of kickstarting the wider UK economy. The much-used cliché, "speculate to accumulate" provides a fitting overview of the situation. Would it not be wise for government to invest in a globally revered product, one that could reap huge financial returns in the future and bring thousands of new jobs to these shores? If redirected properly, the huge profits that our national game generates across a variety of different sectors could be used to stimulate the economy, restitch the fabric of our society and pay back into government coffers. Simply put, our domestic football industry is a huge government investment opportunity in waiting.

A New Political Possibility

Perhaps Oscar Wilde was wrong when he claimed that a cynic "knows the price of everything". Presently, English fandom seems unaware of a rather exciting political prospect: despite their social and cultural importance, our football clubs are *very* cheap. In fact, from a macroeconomic perspective, the entire football industry is rather inconsequential, with revenue totalling just a few billion pounds. Rather advantageously, this makes it easier to nationalise. Firstly, let us focus on the prospect of securing collective ownership of our beloved football clubs. International law requires fair market value compensation when a business is nationalised, so how much would they cost?

Judging an individual football club's financial worth is not an exact science, as there are a number of variables to consider. Essentially, the collective value of our clubs is up for political debate. However, with that being said, according to a rough estimate of market valuations (which are variable), all English football clubs are collectively worth somewhere in the region of £25–30 billion (estimate verified by Kieran Maguire). At state level, this is very affordable. For example, buying every football club in England would cost a similar amount to the recently constructed Elizabeth Line, a small segment of London's sprawling transport network. Incredibly, we could buy our sacred clubs for less than what government paid for the Covid-19 Track and Trace system (which actually turned out to be a glorified spreadsheet worth £37 billion). The controversial HS2 project is now tipped to come in at somewhere around £70 billion, although the overall figure seems to be constantly rising. For perspective, the construction of a much-maligned railway line from Birmingham to London costs over twice the amount of all our football clubs combined. Many politicians are demanding that energy companies become nationalised, which would cost upwards of £400 billion. In fact, energy companies have already been offered in excess of £130 billion for the privilege of continuing to financially exploit the British people.[2] These figures dwarf the cost of the footballing sector and highlight the huge spending power available to the state. In financial terms, football is a very small industry, which is very convenient in terms of planning a public takeover. Therefore, if the political will to spend roughly £25–£30 billion on purchasing our football clubs emerged, the acquisition of these cultural institutions could only be viewed as a financially viable endeavour.

The prospect of achieving fan-ownership of our much-loved football clubs certainly triggers a sense of nervous excitement. But what about the billionaires and consortiums who currently own our clubs — would they not have something to say? Well, this is a question of money and power, which can all be boiled down to one word: politics. Through an Act of Parliament, it's possible to drastically rearrange our domestic football industry from top to bottom. Our elected government sits above all other ruling entities, including football's governing authorities, therefore it is through the mechanism of state intervention that we can dispossess current owners and bring football clubs into public ownership. Brexit certainly helps this process — dispossessed claimants wouldn't exactly be able to appeal via the European Court of Justice. However, in the event of clubs being nationalised, there is one legal avenue that current owners could explore: the European Convention of Human Rights (ECHR), which is an international treaty (not an EU treaty) and therefore unaffected by Brexit — it's been part of UK law since the Human Rights Act 1998.

Article 1 of Protocol 1 of the ECHR guarantees the right to the peaceful enjoyment of property:

> Every natural or legal person is entitled to the peaceful enjoyment of his possessions. No one shall be deprived of his possessions except in the public interest and subject to the conditions provided for by law and by the general principles of international law.[3]

However, this right is not absolute, but qualified, and is therefore removable. States retain the authority to intervene in property rights, providing that any interference is justified by the public interest. Advantageously, states are afforded a "wide margin of appreciation" for interpreting what exactly constitutes "public interest". This legal term acknowledges that different states may have varied cultural, social, and political contexts, and thus permits them a degree of flexibility in interpreting and applying legal standards. Therefore, if a compelling argument can be made for nationalising football clubs "in the public interest" then precedent shows that appeals will not be successful in overturning the decision.

In addressing numerous legal challenges related to nationalisation, the European Court of Human Rights has established two fundamental rules that governments must observe:

- Any interference with the right to property must be in accordance with the law.
- It must strike a fair balance between the individual's right to property and the legitimate goals of the state in the public interest.[4]

Therefore, a compensation scheme would need to fairly evaluate our clubs' financial worth, which could be done by an independent body of specialists. In order to satisfy the ECHR's legal requirements and prevent any future legal challenges from being successful, the figures must be at least slightly over market valuation. According to the estimate above, by offering owners a compensation package at the higher end of market valuation, the state would be paying somewhere in the region of £30 billion to legally acquire ownership rights for all English football clubs. If this transaction was realised through an Act of Parliament, there is absolutely nothing that current club owners could do to prevent it from happening — particularly with government being afforded a "wide margin of appreciation" for acting in the public interest.

But what type of ownership model should be considered? Straightforward nationalisation, such as those undertaken by Labour in the post-war period, is an option. However, this approach would involve a large degree of centralised control and would not be sufficient in democratising football or shifting the balance of power in favour of us. This is because a conventional form of Attlee-inspired nationalisation would enable the government to fully own English football's assets and infrastructure. In this instance, all democratic control of our national game would be lodged firmly within the institutions of the state. Such an approach would not really provide us with any form of power, it would just shift control of English football from big business to the elected government. This would be perhaps the lesser of two evils, but nonetheless an avenue which would still disempower English fandom.

Introducing a Public-Common Partnership

A more appropriate ownership model can be found in a Public-Common Partnership (PCP). As defined by Keir Milburn and Bertie Russell, a PCP represents an alternative ownership model that emphasises joint enterprise between the state and a Common Association (CA). This model is distinct from traditional forms of state ownership, as it introduces a "commons" framework aimed at fostering participatory democracy and decentralised control. The intention is to allow "commoners" (or in this case us) to own and manage resources at the local level.

Initially, ownership rights would be split fairly evenly between us — the Common Association (51%) — and the state (49%). Borrowing from the German club-ownership model, the Common Association would enjoy a majority share, swaying things in our favour. However, the state's 49% share could be reduced over time as the football industry churns out profits and pays back the original government investment. In a scaled operation, the ownership rights of all English football's PCPs could gradually shift towards the Common Association, ending up at say 90%, with the state retaining only a tiny fraction of the overall pie.

Before applying this new model to English football, let's take a look at how standard PCPs operate. Although ownership rights of PCPs are split between just two parties (the state and CA), its democratically-elected board incorporates three separate entities:

The structure of the joint enterprise produces three democratic fora:

1. The state apparatus, where the democratic act is primarily representative electoral politics;
2. The governance of the joint enterprise (comprised of representatives of the local authority, the Common Association, and parties appropriate to the joint enterprise);
3. The Common Association itself, with its own membership and independent mechanisms of participation and decision-making.[5]

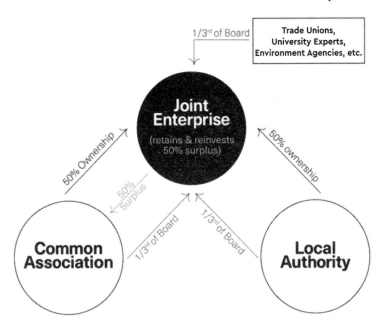

(Image courtesy of Keir Milburn and Bertie Russell)

The concept of a Public-Common Partnership aligns with the idea of creating a balance between public and private interests while ensuring that the community has a say in the governance and utilisation of shared resources. An important principle in the management of PCPs relates to the "rule of subsidiary". This means that all decisions should be made at the most local level possible. That doesn't mean that the most local level — in this case a football club — can decide anything they want. Rather, they would have to make decisions within broad parameters set by entities operating on a wider geographical scale.

What Relationship Should PCPs Have with the State?

The state's role in a PCP is to represent the wider public

interest, but that doesn't necessarily mean that the state would influence all decision-making. As Keir Milburn explains:

> What we've done in other proposals is to use the available legal structures (Community Benefit Societies, etc) to delimit the rights and responsibilities of different parties feeding into a PCP. So, for instance there could be some decisions that the public representative would be excluded from. Or the workers could have increased voting rights for decisions around their terms and conditions etc. So, in my opinion, it would make sense to retain some level of state involvement but to limit its powers and responsibilities.

Therefore, through a PCP model, the power and influence of the state within the geopolitical landscape of English football could be strategically defined and contained. Granted, the state must hold some sway in the governance of domestic football, however this influence would be limited to whatever we as a collective decided upon. For certain decisions, we could practise the principle of subsidiary and grant ourselves full democratic control.

Regardless of the elected government, it would make sense to write a constitution which outlined some basic principles for how English football should be governed. This collectively formulated constitution could provide a reference point for elected leaders to follow and a concrete framework by which to monitor their activities. Without speculating any further on what this constitution should entail, this thesis shall adhere to two obvious principles. The first being that "English football should be managed in a way which best serves the interests of Britain and Her people". The second principle shall be to "protect and enhance English football's position as a dominant worldwide brand". Following these two guiding principles would ensure that English football is governed in a manner which suits the majority and that its overall profits are maintained.

Applying the PCP Model to English Football

Public-Common Partnerships are not fixed institutional forms, rather they can be tailored to suit the demands of a particular situation. Therefore, this model of ownership could be upscaled for the wider movement of shifting English football's related industries into the public sphere. The intention being that we would all become shareholders and by extension joint *owners* of not just our football clubs, but also the wider infrastructure and manufacturing processes that make up the football industry. Therefore, every paying member would join two Common Associations, gaining dual membership of a local and national body. This format would provide two clear avenues of democratic participation. The first would link to the PCP of their chosen football club, and the second would involve a wider PCP affiliated with the entire football industry.

Indeed, transforming football into a public service demands the creation of a huge entity on a national scale involving millions of members. This massive organisation would need to incorporate all ventures related to English football, including a broadcasting service, public gambling company, public brewery, social media platform, replica shirt manufacturing processes and, of course, our clubs. Moreover, football's governing bodies would also need to come under its umbrella. Therefore, all of English football's sources of funding, its governing bodies and our football clubs, would ultimately need to be merged into one giant Public-Common Partnership. For demonstration purposes, we shall label this wider PCP as "EF" (meaning "English Football"). This huge PCP would collate all the profits made in the name of English football and a democratic body would decide what to do with all the money. Essentially it's a Russian doll, with one massive PCP incorporating other national-scale PCPs within it. This would mean that profits made at a national (and international) level would be forced downwards through the principle of subsidiary.

Therefore, operating as a colossal Public-Common Partnership, the entire English football industry would be democratically managed by us (the Common Association), the elected government and an independent body of relevant specialists. Within this macro-structure, a network of smaller PCPs would be incorporated, all relating to the governance, manufacturing and delivery of English football to the wider world. Importantly, within every PCP, a portion of decision-making would be shared with experts in an appropriate field. Indeed, most decision-making would be at the behest of the Common Association, but it's vital that the voices of knowledgeable consultants hold sway because managing and funding football as a public service would require expert advice across a variety of different sectors.

A core element of all PCPs involves the democratic control of profits generated by the joint enterprise. Naturally, a portion of surplus value needs to be reinvested back into achieving the operational goals. This wider public PCP would be responsible for managing the financial landscape of English football, thus ensuring that enough money is pumped back into the system. However, a substantial portion of surplus profits would be pushed downwards into the hands of the

Common Association, or rather us. From there, these profits could be distributed throughout a well-established localised network of smaller PCPs and pumped into communities. Our football clubs represent these smaller PCPs, as they provide the perfect mechanism for democratically distributing wealth throughout our nation.

Football Clubs as PCPs

Because they operate at a local level, the rule of subsidiary can be applied more assertively within our localised football clubs. Members from the Common Association could be incorporated onto the boards of the PCP's other two decision-making entities — the local authority and the joint enterprise. This would ensure that the Common Association becomes the key driver in all decision-making. It would also make sense to have elected members of the local council incorporated onto the board of every club's local authority. This would enable democratically governed football clubs to partially merge with (and influence) local councils, thus granting themselves quicker approvals for land access and development schemes, etc.

In alignment with the model outlined above, football clubs would become the legal property of their supporters, us. Members (or supporters) would be required to pay a monthly fee in order to gain access to voting rights and other services supplied by the club. Democratic procedure would be established, with club boardroom officials elected by the membership base and directly accountable to them. How exactly football clubs would operate under this model is impossible to predict. Would some clubs integrate with local businesses? What about the possibility of merging fully with local councils in order to better improve transport infrastructure and other services? Could strong or weak economic and political alliances be built between clubs? Perhaps experimental structures of power and hierarchy may emerge, who knows? Regulation should protect sporting integrity and fair competition on the pitch, but off it, how members choose to run their football clubs would broadly be up to them. Through the use of Public-Common Partnerships, space for new and interesting modes of governance would likely emerge, with democratic procedure at the heart of every club's decision-making process.

Membership Payments

The Common Association essentially represents us. In order to become a member, British citizenship would be required, or proof of British residency. This legislation would limit the number of possible shareholders and put English football firmly in the hands of English fandom. As a point of principle, the cost of every club membership would be the same throughout the pyramid, from the twelfth tier (or below) to the Premier League. For the purposes of simplicity, we'll determine that membership is priced at £10 a month and paid 12 months of the year. On top of this, an extra charge of £1 a month would be added so that every paying member of a football club also belongs to the wider "EF" PCP as well. Thus meaning, through combined monthly payments totalling £11, English football fans would automatically gain dual membership of both their football club and this new colossal public organisation. Each would be given a democratic vote in deciding wider policies and leadership contests for both PCPs. If a member is unable to afford their subscription programme, then one hour of volunteering per month would suffice. Cheaper rates could be offered for children, the disabled, the unemployed and the elderly.

But what about the millions of English football fans outside of Britain? Is this "British-only" ownership model not a little exclusionary? In order to protect and enhance English football as a dominant worldwide brand, our clubs should be reaching out to supporters in other countries, not excluding them. Therefore it would make sense for English fandom to hand over a small percentage of ownership rights to supporters outside of England.

If we were willing to hand over 10% ownership rights of our football clubs to supporters in other countries, then the financial benefits would be huge. Although still excluded from the wider "EF" PCP, these supporters could be charged a very affordable £1 a month subscription fee, meaning that they're incorporated into an individual club's Common Association. They could then be given a democratic voice in a club's decision-making, albeit to a lesser extent than full members. Part-membership would include regular email correspondence, the chance to vote on certain club policies and also inclusion within English football's social media platform. Therefore, for just £1 a month, these fans could engage directly with English fandom online and enjoy a genuine stake in our longstanding cultural heritage.

Allowing 10% of our football clubs to be owned like this would serve the two basic principles mentioned earlier. This is because such a policy would enhance English football as a global brand by drawing in hundreds of millions of fans on an emotional level. And with annual membership payments of £12, it would also do so financially. If this money was invested properly, it could be used to benefit British society as a whole. In order to understand the huge amounts of riches that this ownership structure could potentially generate, let's consider (arguably) our most globally revered club, Manchester United. According to market research firm Kantar, the Red Devils have over 650 million fans worldwide.[6] If 500 million of these global fans decided to pay just £1 month in membership fees, then £6 billion every season would be transferred into Manchester United's coffers. Perhaps these supporter figures are exaggerated, but if their 80 million plus dedicated followers on Facebook all decided to invest in the club, then £960 million would be generated on an annual basis. Even erring on the side of caution, this huge financial figure dwarfs typical sponsorship deals. For context, Manchester United's recent shirt deal with Team Viewer in 2022 was the most lucrative in the Premier League at the time, netting them £48 million that season (a mere 5% of the previous figure).

Under such a scheme, it would be in the interests of every club to appeal to fans in other countries, as this would expand the membership base and increase profits. A collectively owned worldwide digital broadcasting service could incorporate a club's own individual TV channel which could then be used to engage with these supporters too. Obviously, the social media platform would offer another direct line of communication. So instead of promoting corporate interests (as they do now), players may be asked to read out messages in other languages as clubs attempt to promote themselves to targeted countries or cultures across the world. Your club's top striker attempting to speak Chinese might be a strange thought. However, approximately 400 million people make up the Chinese middle class, and if a message resonated with a tiny percentage of them, then millions of pounds of extra income could potentially come flowing into the bank account of your club every season.

Overseas subscribers are now the main contributor to English football's riches. Therefore by bringing them in closer and offering them a genuine stake in the English game, we would be ensuring their long-term financial commitment to a huge corporate structure that we own.

Changing the Wider Political Landscape

If Public-Common Partnerships came to define English football's entire structure of governance, then the ramifications of such a transition would extend far beyond the sporting realm. This model would devolve power and influence away from a cartel of unelected corporate players by spreading democratic ownership throughout the wider economy. Indeed, by gaining collective control of several large corporations, spanning a variety of different sectors, English fandom would be awarding itself a lot of political clout. In turn, this would weaken a number of overseas billionaires' growing stranglehold on our public discourse. Through the collective ownership of an international broadcasting service and a social media platform, we would be severely diminishing their political sphere of influence. For example, who would bother subscribing to SKY or TNT? How many millions would abandon X (formally known as Twitter) or Facebook in favour of a platform whereby algorithms were transparently programmed, bots were eradicated, personal data was protected and rules of engagement were democratically decided? Shifting the balance of power from private to public, PCPs would partially democratise the media landscape of Britain, much to the frustration of the current establishment.

Furthermore, through the collective power of the Common Association, English fandom would have the potential to lobby and influence central government. Presently, such lobbying takes place in the shadows at the behest of corporate entities. However, this gigantic PCP would become one of the most powerful corporations in the UK, thus granting us a new form of economic and political influence. True, coordinating an institution involving millions of people would be fraught with logistical issues. But this would be a nice problem to have. Modern communications technology is capable of hosting mass engagement via democratic forums and aligning interests through online referendums. Yes, people are becoming increasingly politically polarised here in the UK, but through the collective ownership of English football, we could begin to understand that there is more in common than that which divides us.

Implementing a collective ownership model is the only solution to combating the ills of a privatised agenda which continues to undermine the beautiful game. Moreover, this political transition presents a number of huge financial benefits. Keeping the production of broadcasting, gambling, alcohol, social media and shirt manufacturing in-house would eradicate billionaires from the system, thus meaning *we* control all the profits ourselves. Additionally, by opening up each club's membership base to overseas subscribers, we could produce levels of funding never seen before in the history of football. Through the principle of subsidiary, all financial decision-making could be devolved to the lowest level possible, thus providing a louder democratic voice to English fandom. In the midst of a failing economic system which continues to ignore the wants of everyday people, the integration of Public-Common Partnerships within our national economy makes perfect political sense, and the football sector is a good place to start.

A Theoretical Funding Model

Physics teaches you to reason from first principles rather than by analogy.

— Elon Musk

Quoting one of the world's wealthiest businessmen provides an ironic twist to our narrative. This is because transforming the football industry into a public service requires the complete removal of billionaires from the economic system. However, that doesn't mean we can't follow their blueprints for success or find inspiration in their practices. After all, our aim is to generate billions of pounds worth of profit.

At the turn of the century, Elon Musk had a problem. He wanted to launch himself into orbit, but soon discovered that aerospace manufacturers charged a lot of money for completed space rockets. Unfortunately, they were simply too expensive. Breaking the problem down using first principles thinking, he came up with a cost-effective solution. Instead of purchasing completed rockets, he realised that it was far cheaper to buy materials directly from the marketplace and manufacture them independently. Therefore, by establishing his own company and cutting out the middleman, Musk found a way to finance his expedition into space. Food for thought. Could the process of first principles thinking help to theoretically fund football as a public service? Well, it's not exactly rocket science.

Football as a service cannot afford to be polluted by commercial or private interests as they've proven to be wholly counterproductive. Therefore, our aim is to create as much profit as possible without the need for any private investment or unwanted commercialism. So what does the logic of first principle thinking dictate? A rational thought process is one that assumes full control of supply-side economics by ceasing any wasteful outsourcing of production. The methodology is clear: English football should create its own manufacturing sector and sell its product directly to the worldwide marketplace. Throughout the supply chain, external companies should be bypassed in order to streamline the business model and create maximum returns. Obviously, individual profiteers must be cut out completely. Therefore, these manufacturing companies must be collectively owned (which is where our model differs from Musk's) and fully dedicated towards financing football as a public service.

Broadcasting

Reimagining the Premier League's broadcasting system is the perfect place to start. Currently, there are a number of external companies involved as TV rights are sold off to the highest bidder in a fractured and inefficient model. The vast majority of Premier League broadcasters around the world are traditional media companies that buy the rights to show live games in a particular market or region. These media companies then assume full responsibility for the production of the programming and the marketing of the product. Over recent decades, BSKYB and BT Sport (now TNT) have cornered the UK broadcasting market and bled us dry with rip-off price hikes. Today, if you want to (legally) watch Premier League football, you're forced to buy a TV package which includes terrible movies and a host of other channels you're simply not interested in watching.

However, the Premier League broadcasting goalposts have shifted — British football fans no longer generate most of the income. As English football reigns supreme on a global scale, it's now the international markets which determine future growth. Indeed, the broadcasting focus may be shifting towards overseas markets, but that's not all that's changing. Over three decades since its launch, satellite television is still king, however a new pretender to the throne awaits. It appears that the next revolution in football broadcasting has arrived, although our all too reactive governing bodies are yet to realise its potential. In 2019, Amazon Prime bought the rights to a small number of Premier League games and on December 3rd of that year, a turning point in broadcasting history occurred. For the first time ever, live Premier League football was legally streamed via the internet, and a new era of televised football had begun — the digital age.

Bring Broadcasting into the Twenty-First Century

For live sport, the future is digital and the major players are already in the market. This shows, if nothing else, that it's possible to stream live sport to a global audience, direct to consumers. With Amazon's foray into Premier League broadcasting, the streaming technology passed its first test. Overall, the quality of coverage was good, and the technology will only improve. Amazon kept things simple, hiring well-known pundits, anchors and commentators, whilst offering a wide choice of games to watch. Consumer feedback was positive — Amazon received a record number of new subscribers as a direct result of their Premier League coverage.[1]

So instead of selling all the TV rights, could the Premier League establish its own independent production company? There is a reason why media outlets are willing to pay billions of pounds for the rights — English football is very popular. The idea that the Premier League should cut out media middlemen is not a new one. Nick Harris is a well-respected football journalist who has been theorising a new broadcasting model for a number of years, and it's one which could completely revolutionise the financial landscape of English football. I contacted Nick and asked him to outline exactly what this prospective model entails. Our discussions took place in 2022 so the figures are the most up to date at that time. Nick explains:

> From writing about these issues for more than 20 years and following the industry closely, I know that around 200m people (or households) currently pay a broadcaster to get access to PL live games. In the UK that figure is around 9m people who pay either Sky or TNT or Amazon to get some or all of the live games. In many countries that figure might be hundreds or thousands of households, or low millions. But they all add up. And typically, they're paying for bundles of content where quite probably the thing they value most is the live football. However, they're paying £30–£60 to have that as part of a wider package of content they might well not want.

The scenario is one in which the Premier League has a direct-to-customer service in which every single game is live and there is a huge archive of matches and goals — all at a cost of say £10 per month. Both the technology and the customer base exist — approximately 200 million people are already paying significantly more for additional content that may be of minimal interest to them. At £10 per month, the Premier League's income potentially becomes £2 billion per month, or £24 billion per year. Cutting the cost of subscriptions might actually increase revenue: at say £5 a month, might the 200 million customers now become 300 million or 500 million? For such a low price, huge amounts of new customers might be in the market for a reliable, legal way to watch all the action.

By outsourcing production to external broadcasters, the Premier League is losing out on vast amounts of potential revenue. Presently, the popularity of English football as a worldwide brand is unrivalled and has a very large captive audience. England is revered as the historical home of football, something no other country can lay claim to, which provides us with a unique advantage in the global market. Not to mention the fast-paced, entertaining nature of our game and the global status of our biggest clubs. The 200 million people who already pay TV subscriptions to access live Premier League games are joined by many others who access them via free terrestrial TV channels or illegal streaming websites. Moreover, with only one broadcasting source available, illegal online hackers would be severely hampered. It's very difficult to hack Netflix or Amazon Prime, and so it would be for PLTV (or whatever we decided to call it). Therefore, without access to illegal streaming sites, it's highly likely that even more punters would sign up to a monthly subscription fee, particularly if it was reasonably priced. The current broadcasting black-out on Saturday afternoons would be lifted, with every Premier League game made available to watch.

The cost of subscription would need to be carefully thought out. That is not to say that £10 a month is necessarily the correct price point, as it would certainly differ across various markets. But there could be multiple options for subscribers to interact with the service, such as paying £2 per game or perhaps £5 for a highlights package. The salient point being that by going direct to consumers, the Premier League could earn significantly more money by giving fans significantly more content. Moreover, this could be achieved by charging far less than traditional legacy broadcasters.

Obviously, the idea is not without hurdles. Building and maintaining a tech platform capable of serving hundreds of millions of customers worldwide would be no mean feat. The Premier League would need to change from being a competition organiser that banks TV rights cheques into a global broadcasting company. However, there is also the option of outsourcing this task to an already established tech giant. As Nick explains:

> One of the tech giants, whether Amazon or Apple (now in bed with MLS to broadcast their games) or Google or Facebook could easily afford to buy all the PL's rights for the next, say, 10 years, for, say, £50bn. And then potentially make £24bn per year in revenues over those 10 years. Would a joint venture work, between the PL and one of those giants? It's entirely feasible. But the idea that rights income has peaked and can't ever get higher ignores the technological possibilities of delivering more to fans, for less, while making more money for the clubs in the process.

Initially, outsourcing production to an already established tech giant would be a less complex affair because these huge corporate entities have vast infrastructures and administrative programs already in place. However, such a decision would prove costly in the long run. Not only would English football lose out financially, as vast amounts of profits are sucked out of the system, but customers would also fall victim to price hikes at the discretion of the contractor. Essentially, we would be in the same position as we are now. If the Premier League were to sell broadcasting rights to a tech giant, it would hand power over to a billionaire cartel. And we already know how this story ends: relentless advertising campaigns, rampant commercialisation and rising prices, but this time with a new twenty-first-century twist — the mass storage of our personal data. The likes of Google, Amazon, Apple and Facebook are becoming increasingly influential, more so than any companies in the history of the world, distorting democratic procedure and controlling the all-important digital realm. It would be a huge mistake to hand any of these corporate behemoths even more power.

If building a single worldwide digital broadcasting platform is such a brilliant idea, then an obvious question springs to mind — why isn't it already in operation? With so much money sitting on the table, why hasn't a huge corporate firm like Amazon or Apple stumped up the cash to buy all the Premier League's TV rights and resell them to a global market? I contacted an ex-employee of a major British broadcaster who has rigorously researched the validity of executing such a proposal. He wishes to remain anonymous. Although my source admits that creating a single worldwide digital broadcasting service is possible, he is sceptical about its chances of success in the private sector.

The major stumbling block is that football's TV rights are in fact overvalued. Effectively, the Premier League is a loss-leader for almost every company that buys the broadcasting rights. For example, SKY paid £1.2 billion per year to supply approximately six million subscribers, which equates to charging £17 a month per household in order to break even. However, SKY only charged £18 per month, which then reduced to just £15 after VAT. So why did SKY bother doing this if they're losing money? Herein lies the catch. As previously noted, subscribers are forced to buy an extra £40+ worth of meaningless SKY products to acquire the Premier League package. These products then generate an additional £1.4 billion in revenue each year. This loss-leading model is applied across the board. BT Sport gave away Premier League football for free. Why? Because you had to buy a high-end broadband product to access it. Basically, companies have been willing to pay over the odds to gain a competitive advantage in the broadcasting marketplace. Live Premier League football has proven to be so popular that punters are willing to jump through hoops in order to watch it, and if that means switching broadband suppliers or buying a host of sub-standard movies, then they'll do it. This is where the profit is made.

But why haven't potential buyers such as Amazon or Apple extracted this loss-leading benefit on a global scale? As my source explains:

Well, first of all they don't have the infrastructure to produce and distribute that volume of content to that many geographical locations with their local regulatory requirements, legal terms and conditions and multilingual customer service requirements. However, the current local buyers do. Secondly, and most importantly, they don't know how to market and sell sports content in those markets. How do you get customer sign ups in places like Indonesia or Taiwan? The local players have been doing this for years, it's their core business — they have all the knowledge and expertise necessary. Apple and Amazon don't want to have to hire teams in Johannesburg, Sydney and Hamburg to help navigate the vagaries of the local markets.

Undoubtedly, creating a worldwide digital broadcasting service would require vast amounts of funding and expertise. Setting up the infrastructure would be costly and my source estimates that you'd need to spend around £200 million on staffing and legal costs before you'd even launched. Furthermore, ongoing operational costs would be somewhere in the region of £500 million a year (100–150 million for producing and distributing the content, 100–150 million for staff and legal, and 200–300 million on marketing and informing people how to sign up for the service). But without question, the biggest financial outlay would be purchasing the TV rights. These are owned by the Premier League and currently worth somewhere between £3–4 billion a year. Therefore, investing in a worldwide digital broadcasting service is risky — that is, if you're a private firm.

But what if you're operating from outside those parameters? What if your company is backed by gargantuan state resources and already owns the TV rights anyhow? In this context, the financial risk is considerably lessened and investing in the needed infrastructure becomes a rational choice. Moreover, a state-backed venture can borrow at far cheaper rates compared to any private contractor. With the annual cost of TV rights being £0, a state-backed Premier League broadcasting model would have a huge competitive advantage in the initial set-up stage that no private firm could lay claim to. Indeed, if Amazon or Apple were granted permission to avoid paying the Premier League for TV rights, then this theoretical broadcasting service would already be in existence in the private sphere (as it is in the MLS).

As it stands, English football is missing out on vast amounts of potential revenue because its fractured broadcasting model is stuck in the twentieth century and geared towards creating profit for private shareholders. But it doesn't need to stay this way. Imagine a publicly owned digital streaming platform selling Premier League football directly to the rest of the world, generating gargantuan profits. A global monopoly working for us.

But is there a way in which English fandom itself could independently help fund this new public service? If we consider our favourite pastimes in relation to football and the consumer revenue streams they produce, then the answer is yes. The intention here is to grow publicly owned companies in targeted industries and allow them to compete alongside privately owned firms. There are two very profitable industries which are deeply embedded within English footballing culture: alcohol and gambling. Let's start by considering the former.

A Public Brewery

Millions of us enjoy a drink whilst watching a game. What if a public brewery was established with the intention of funnelling all profits directly into the service of football? A nationally owned brewery might seem like a wild idea to many, but we only have to look to our own recent past to see that something like this has already happened. The Carlisle State Management scheme was introduced in 1916 as a way of regulating the pubs in and around the Gretna munitions factory and was vital to the war effort. This brought pubs in the area under national control and imposed a set of rules and regulations on them. It also meant that the pubs were modernised to include outdoor areas with games and activities, whilst advertising was limited. As the people that ran them weren't motivated by money-making, the need to sell vast amounts of alcohol was reduced. The question of the alcohol industry's relationship to excessive drinking is an ongoing one, and taking the need to make a profit out of alcohol has all kinds of benefits and savings further down the line in terms of medical care, absenteeism and public order issues. There is speculation as to why the scheme both ended and lasted so long, one is that it made a profit every year for the government and it was only the Thatcherite ideology of privatisation that meant the legislation was repealed.

There are a number of ways a brewery system could work, with the scale of the operation dependent upon a number of different factors, none more so than the quality of the final products. However, for demonstration purposes only, let us assume that a collectively owned public brewery manages to develop a delightfully refreshing lager, a classy pale ale and a particularly smooth bitter. Three different types of alcoholic beverage, offering punters a variety of choice as they scan the bar taps on match day. Clearly, some clever branding would be required in order to associate these products with the service of football. Perhaps "The People's Lager" or "The People's Pale Ale" would suffice? Or perhaps you can tell that I don't work in advertising. The point being that a publicly owned brewery would supply drinks to football stadiums and surrounding licensed premises. Therefore, as fans walk into their favourite pub for a pre-match tipple, they would be given the option of buying a drink that they know contributes to the betterment of English football. Assuming the product is of a decent standard, then millions of football fans across the country would likely enjoy purchasing these alcoholic beverages on a regular basis. In turn, this would produce profits that would be recycled straight from the pockets of football fans and back into the service of football. I'll drink to that.

Potentially, the products created by this publicly owned brewery may begin to establish themselves more and more within the wider marketplace. As a result, production could be scaled up to supply pubs, clubs, restaurants and other establishments throughout the whole country. Moreover, our digital broadcasting service could be used as a mechanism to advertise these alcoholic beverages not only to us, but also to millions of subscribers across the globe. Could our brewery even begin to imitate the local products of various other countries in an attempt to compete on an international scale? As previously referenced, the size of the operation would depend upon the quality of the goods produced, but controlling what is advertised through our broadcasting service channels affords us with an opportunity. If PLTV exclusively advertised only our products, it would provide a huge competitive advantage in the wider marketplace. We know that advertising works, and if it's used to create money for a public service then the ends would justify the means.

Another option would be to establish a network of local microbreweries that would supply their nearest grounds and surrounding pubs, as opposed to one major manufacturer distributing the same products. This approach would celebrate our local quirks and differences and provide a larger variety of beverages. Consequently, this would enhance the chances of one of them establishing a foothold in the wider marketplace (both domestic and international).

There are a number of different ways that this scheme could potentially operate, perhaps a combination of microbreweries working alongside a major manufacturer might work best? Could some football clubs even work with local breweries to establish their own unique brands? With so many options to consider, let the principle of the idea be our focal point. Establishing a publicly owned brewery would allow us to recycle some of the money we spend on our favourite pastime.

A Public Gambling Company

Now let's shift our focus over to the hugely profitable betting industry. In order to grasp just how lucrative modern gambling firms have become, it's worth considering the wealth of Denise Coates, founder of UK-based betting firm Bet365. Over the course of the last two decades, she has acquired a fortune worth an estimated £6.2 billion. In 2020, she awarded herself a record-breaking annual salary of £421 million, supplemented by £48 million in dividends.[2] The fortune earned by Denise Coates is evidence that owning a gambling company makes you incredibly rich. Although this may seem like an extremely obvious point to make, there is a rather obvious question that we are yet to ask ourselves off the back of it. Why don't we establish a collectively owned gambling company?

But before we get there, we should again challenge the idea that the way we do things now is the way we have always done them. We have had a national betting company before, for horse racing. The Tote or the Horserace Totalisator Board, was set up in 1928 by, of all people, Winston Churchill — who no one would accuse of being a socialist — and then privatised by Jack Straw and the Blair government who supposedly were. The purpose of the board was to make sure that money from betting was put back into racing and to offer an alternative to illegal off-course betting. It operated by pooling money from punters' bets, and after winnings were paid, any profits were put back into the racing industry. By the time it was privatised, the Tote had an estimated value of £200 million, around 280 high-street betting shops, operated on-course outlets and made about £12 million a year, with £10 million ploughed back into racing.

Both Norway and Finland, two of our highly developed European neighbours, have national gambling companies, Norsk Tipping and Veikkaus respectively. Both models are coming under pressure from the rise of online gambling and other commercial interests, but the idea is a nationally owned gambling company. This isn't to say that we should copy these models, rather we should come up with new ones.

In fact, a publicly owned gambling company is already in operation, and over the years it's proven to be a huge success. The National Lottery generates billions annually for the British population, supporting fledgling local businesses and funding myriad schemes that improve the lives of many people. Therefore we already know that the concept of a public gambling company works in practice, the only challenge would be to apply it in a slightly different manner.

It makes a lot of sense to establish a public gambling website which offers exactly the same betting services as traditional private firms. This collectively owned company could then mirror any new innovations and compete alongside them in the marketplace. Digital platforms have revolutionised the gaming industry, and it has grown exponentially since the turn of the century. In 2018, the gross gambling revenue in the UK alone was approximately £14.4 billion.[3] The fact that a lot of these profits often end up in the offshore bank accounts of wealthy individuals is a crying shame. Not only does this practice undermine the UK gambling landscape, it also reduces funds reinvested into society. Furthermore, it means that football is used for corporate gain, without getting a decent slice of the financial benefits itself — an all too familiar story.

Once again, collective ownership of football's broadcasting would prove to be very useful in supporting this scheme. If the broadcasting service was to only advertise our public betting firm, then it would provide it with a huge competitive advantage. Moreover, if shirt sponsorship was banned, then the traditional betting firms who currently dominate the UK gambling industry would find that the football industry had completely shut them out. In this reality, not a single betting slogan or logo would appear on our screens during a football match — apart from the one that makes us money. But why stick with just one public betting firm? Multiple public betting companies could potentially be established in order to increase market share, though we would need to be careful about drowning punters in advertising once again. There is also the option of leveraging a simple windfall tax upon private gambling operators who offer football betting odds to the UK population. The idea is simple: restructure the gambling industry in order to transfer as much wealth as possible from the offshore bank accounts of billionaires into the public service of football.

However, it's no secret that thousands of people in the UK develop gambling problems. Stricter regulation now requires betting firms to assume more social responsibility for the ills produced by gambling, but, nevertheless, if punters quit, they're often bombarded with offers in a bid to entice them back. Private firms are all about producing profits for shareholders, and the compulsive activities of addicted gamblers can help achieve that aim. Current regulation has proven to be ineffective in solving the problem, as slogans placed at the end of advertising campaigns will achieve very little in the way of rehabilitation. Certainly, more needs to be done. In fact, targeting a reduction in addicts should be at the centre of a public gambling company's policy, with increased resources made available for identifying and assisting vulnerable punters. Gambling can ruin lives, however making it illegal would be counterproductive. An unregulated black market would emerge, offering no protection whatsoever to those with addiction problems. Prohibition has not stopped drugs such as cannabis or cocaine from flooding our streets, and it certainly didn't work with alcohol in the US. In reality, such a measure would only push gambling underground — this is not a viable option. With millions of punters enjoying responsible gambling throughout the UK, the most practical solution is to structure and control the market in a manner that best suits the country as a whole.

A publicly owned gambling company should be established for British punters to enjoy, safe in the knowledge that when the house wins, their money is being used to improve football, not line the pockets of billionaires. The funds generated could serve to support local club community projects and help pay for the thousands of jobs created by the movement of football into the public sector. In this way, the establishment of a nationalised gambling company would not only boost profits, but also catalyse a huge investment in our civic and economic sectors. Will the punters of Britain choose to put their money into a website that effectively funds the footballing pyramid? It's surely worth the gamble (pun intended). Our stakes would be paying the wages of the talent we're betting on, the epitome of a self-sustaining economic model.

Replica Shirt Manufacturing
People all around the globe love buying replica jerseys of English football teams. The likes of Manchester United, Liverpool, Arsenal and Manchester City regularly compete

with a small selection of other European giants on the international market. In any given season, English teams will make up a significant number of the top ten best-selling club football kits around the world. In the UK, replica jerseys are also incredibly popular — it's difficult to walk along any busy high street without seeing at least one shirt on your travels. So how does this very lucrative business operate? Presently, shirt production is outsourced to private companies such as Nike and Adidas. As Daniel Geey explains in his book *Done Deal*, it appears that our football clubs are being short-changed:

> Kit manufacturers usually take 80–90% of all revenue from shirt sales. Clubs in return receive large, "up-front" payments from their kit manufacturer. At best, the club can earn 20% of all net sales, though for many large deals, such royalty payments to a club only kick in once a large number of sales have already been made.[4]

Therefore, at best clubs are receiving a paltry one-fifth of shirt sales revenue. Adidas's most recent deal with Manchester United is reportedly worth £750 million over a ten-season period. This eye-watering sum may look great at first glance, but, considering Adidas's own forecasting model assumes the club will generate shirt sales in excess of £1.5 billion within that same period, it suddenly appears rather meagre.[5]

Corporate sports giants such as Adidas and Nike are extracting millions of pounds from the English game on an annual basis. The majority of their manufacturing takes place in Asia where workers are paid low wages. In 2018, the *Telegraph* reported that the workers making England's £160 World Cup shirts in Bangladesh were being paid 21p an hour.[6]

Could this system of exploitation be altered? Instead of each individual football club selling their rights to private firms, is there another way to manage the business of making and selling replica jerseys? Obviously, most football clubs don't have the operational capacity to set up localised shirt production and distribution facilities. However, with a GDP of over £2 trillion, our state does. And with a readymade international market of willing consumers, this state investment has the potential to prove to be a lucrative venture in the long term.

If a network of factories were to be established across the country, installed to accommodate a new, booming shirt manufacturing enterprise, thousands of new jobs would be produced in our domestic manufacturing sector, thus contributing a degree of balance to an economy overly reliant on finance and services. A government-led programme which invested heavily in such a scheme would soon see the UK reap significant financial and societal benefits. Initially setting up a network of factories would be a costly venture, but, over the course of time, a collectively owned shirt manufacturing company could create huge amounts of profit.

Furthermore, owning our shirt production processes would mean that we can design our team's kits ourselves, rather than relying on the (often underwhelming) efforts of global sports corporations. Although each football club would be responsible for the design of its own kits, this huge corporation would have a small logo printed onto every shirt it made, a recognisable emblem that represented English football and English fandom as a whole.

Indeed, taking football into the public sector would allow us to establish our own shirt production mechanisms, and moreover take 100% of the profits. Some of our biggest clubs are selling over one million shirts a season, which highlights the scale of the potential opportunity. Presently, half of the world's top ten shirt sellers are made up of English teams, yet people are buying these jerseys because they support the club, not Nike or Adidas, an obvious yet important distinction to make. Obviously, production costs would be upped considerably if shirts were to be made on British soil. However, to compensate for this, the operation could be run as a non-profit. Such a scheme would save hundreds of millions of pounds by not paying private shareholders their usual gains. Establishing thousands of local jobs and balancing the scales of the wider economy would be profit enough. There is also the option of outsourcing a certain percentage of production facilities to countries where manufacturing costs are lower (whilst still paying reasonable wages).

Therefore, in order to further control the economic landscape of our national sport, the service of football should establish a huge replica shirt manufacturing corporation. There are still of course a host of questions unanswered about the finer details. Could we scale down production to a level that suited us and our planet better, perhaps creating a new kit design once every two or three seasons? Exactly how much production would need to take place abroad in order to balance the books? There are too many possibilities to consider at this stage of proceedings, but the premise is simple: we assume control of everything. In doing so, we control not just the economic landscape but also the moral compass of such business ventures. Perhaps this whole chapter can be summarised by adding a new word to Nike's famous slogan, "Just do it *ourselves*".

Controlling the Market

Agents run the game.

Alan Sugar

Creating a new economic model that pumps billions of pounds into English football would be pointless if it all went on player wages. But without effective regulation in place, this is exactly what would happen. Throughout footballing history, clubs have always sought to spend their way to success. Even when football was an amateur sport, clubs were using the "expenses" loophole to pay players. We've been bending the rules since the 1880s, as everybody wants their team to be competitive and win silverware. It's a constant merry-go-round of one-upmanship because the will to win is encoded into our DNA. Hypothetically, if a club spent £2 billion on player wages and won the league, then rival fans would be demanding that their club spend even more than that next season — so up and up the wage bills would go. This circumstance becomes inevitable under free market economics, and it's exactly the situation we find ourselves in today. Without effective regulation, wealthy clubs become locked in an unrestrained arms race to sign the world's best players, resulting in widespread debt, financial misdemeanours and monopolisation. Therefore, if the aim is to make clubs profitable, simplify the financial landscape and create a more competitive top flight, then the best solution is to control the market.

However, this creates a new problem. What if controlling the market undermines the quality of players plying their trade in the Premier League? Top players may be drawn to other leagues which pay higher wages, and this would compromise a core principle of the proposed constitution — protecting and enhancing English football's position as a worldwide brand. Moving forward, it's imperative that the Premier League retains a high number of elite players in order to appeal to the rest of the world. So, controlling the market becomes a balancing act, and a tricky tightrope to walk. But if it can be done successfully, then the benefits to English football, and English society, would be huge.

So how do we successfully navigate this metaphorical tightrope? First of all, it's important to establish some basic values in terms of what we want any new regulation to achieve. These guiding principles are the long stick that a tightrope walker holds on to in order to maintain balance. In this context, there is no right or wrong *per se*, simply an opinion or a vision of how we believe football should be governed. Obviously, the following recommendations cannot speak for the collective us at this stage, rather the intention is to simply suggest an example of one possible future model.

Effective regulation needs to be kept simple. Boiled down to four core principles, English football should be governed in a manner that:

- Promotes sporting integrity and fair competition.
- Creates profit.
- Ensures that world-class players play for English teams.
- Promotes local talent.

Arguably, the vast majority of English fandom would agree that these principles form a solid foundation from which to build an effective regulatory system. As a general rule of thumb, we all enjoy the spectacle of a competitive league and everybody likes making profit. However, there is also a paradoxical element to our relationship with football — an innate desire to watch the world's best players perform, coupled with a sense of loyalty to the local players who we want to see do well. But this paradox should not necessarily be viewed as a problem, instead it should be seen as an opportunity. It's all about striking the right balance on the pitch by fusing a vast array of elite foreign talent with a good smattering of home-grown local lads. Although these four principles do overlap with some contemporary sloganeering, the intention here is to take them seriously, turning lip service into meaningful regulatory action.

If these core values are to be upheld, then there is one form of regulation that must be implemented — a wage cap. Simply put, some kind of ceiling on spending power has to be imposed, otherwise, hyper wage inflation is inevitable. As previously mentioned, if free market principles are given free reign, then richer clubs will concentrate elite players into giant squads and debt becomes unavoidable. However, a poorly implemented wage cap could threaten the core principle of ensuring that world class players sign for English clubs, and this would diminish the quality of our top division. Therefore, this type of regulation needs to be carefully considered.

At first glance, the question about whether to re-install a wage cap may feel like a 'Catch-22' situation, as in, we're damned if we do and damned if we don't. But on closer inspection, this isn't necessarily the case. There are ways around the potential problem of a wage cap lowering the standard of our top flight.

The most obvious answer is to keep Premier League wage bills incredibly high, thus meaning our clubs can easily compete for the signatures of elite players. But there is also a second safeguard, and an interesting example of which is provided by Major League Soccer (MLS) in the United States.

Despite being fanatical followers of neoliberalism in the wider economy, the US abandons free market ideology when it comes to regulating its sporting competitions. In fact, it would be difficult to describe their systems as anything other than socialist. The very fact that US sporting institutions do not allow neoliberalism to distort their sporting political landscape is most definitely a lesson for us, and it relates to the first core principle listed above. So if we were to regulate the market, how could we walk the tightrope of controlling wage inflation whilst still attracting world-class talent to our shores?

The Designated Player Rule

Imposing a wage cap does not necessarily mean that big spenders would be fully restricted — there is a potential loophole. Over in the United States, their MLS format operates under an entirely different system and its methods offer a relevant case study. The MLS operates under a single-entity structure with centralised management of player contracts. Instead of traditional club owners, the league features "investor- operators", each serving as a shareholder in the league. This setup guarantees that clubs are owned collectively by the MLS, rather than by independent individuals with private interests. All revenues generated are pooled centrally and subsequently redistributed to the participating teams through a centralised mechanism. Furthermore, there are complex rules and regulations regarding player transfers, which ensure that a particular set of wealthy clubs aren't able to drastically outspend the rest of the competition. Since its establishment in 1996, the MLS has implemented a wage cap. However, from 2007, the "Designated Player Rule" (created to facilitate the signing of David Beckham) has permitted each club to sign three players exempt from the league's wage limit parameters.

Could this piece of legislation be applied in England? An MLS-inspired Designated Player Rule would still permit the presence of marquee transfer deals in the Premier League, but a salary cap would work in tandem with it, safeguarding the notion of fair competition and preventing clubs from overspending. This guidance would provide a certain degree of flexibility to an otherwise rigid salary cap, making room for the massive wage demands of world-class performers and thus ensuring that the Premier League retains its stature as an elite competition. Therefore, a segment of regulation would allow free market economics to operate, but only to a certain extent. Clubs would have the option of spending some of their own commercial gains (accrued from membership payments, player sales and merchandise sales, etc.) in the transfer market, although it would need to be capped at a certain percentage. This would prevent clubs from irresponsibly spending more money than they could afford on player wages. In order to ensure that boardroom officials play with a straight bat, clubs would be responsible for publicly displaying their balance sheets in a perfectly transparent financial system, thus providing proof of funds for every player bought under the Designated Player Rule.

Allowing a small number of players to be bought outside the limitations of a wage cap would offer an inviting compromise for those with reservations about imposing such a system.

Moreover, the Designated Player Rule does not necessarily have to be reserved exclusively for three players, as the number could be raised or reduced. It's a fluid concept and the exact details would need to be democratically decided upon.

This combination of MLS-based regulation would strike a nice balance in supporting three of our essential core principles. The Designated Player Rule would ensure that our clubs could meet the huge wage demands of elite, world-class talent, whilst an overarching salary cap underpins two objectives. Firstly, it would limit club spending, and therefore bring about the possibility of creating profit. Secondly, there is historical evidence to suggest that it would create a more competitive nature in our top flight.

Bring Back the Salary Cap

In order to quash the rising wage inflation of the late Victorian era, the FA imposed a weekly salary cap in 1901. It lasted sixty years, before Jimmy Hill's band of reformers had it lifted in 1961. With 125 completed seasons of English league football under our belt to date, the abolition of the wage cap intercepts this period of time at near enough the halfway point — 63 years ago. Using the beginning of the twentieth century as a starting point (1901), we can divide English football league history into two segments. The first, lasting 60 years, where the wage cap was in place, and the other lasting 63 years, without any wage cap whatsoever. So has the removal of a salary cap made a difference to the competitive nature of our top division?

Under the imposition of a wage cap, over a 60-year period, 19 different clubs were crowned champions of England. But in the second segment, after the wage cap was lifted, this figure reduces to just 13. Over roughly the same time period, a deregulated transfer market has reduced the number of different teams winning the league by 32%. To date, 24 different clubs have been crowned champions of England. Is this the final figure? Are we at the end of history? Perhaps so, because without proper regulation, the rest of the pack cannot compete adequately with the wealthiest clubs. As a general rule, the club which spends the most on wages usually wins the league. How could anyone argue that such a system is worthy of governing any sporting competition?

Yet more evidence reveals that a salary cap enhances competitiveness. In May 2023, shortly after Manchester City bulldozed their way to a third straight Premier League title, the *Athletic* published a graph showing winning streaks of ten games (or more) for clubs competing in England's top-flight. The author of the piece, Duncan Alexander, rightly claimed that "Manchester City did not start the trend of big runs of consecutive wins in the English top-flight", but he failed to mention what stopped them. During their emergence in the 1890s, there wasn't any wage regulation in place; however, after the implementation of a salary cap, no team managed a single ten-game winning streak over the course of five decades. In the decade it was lifted, the 1960s, the consecutive ten-game winning streaks began once again.[1] Clearly, these huge winning streaks are becoming increasingly common. In the century from 1890 to 1990, instances of teams winning ten games in a row in England's top flight occurred on just nine occasions. The Premier League has seen 11 in the previous 14 years alone. It doesn't take a genius to work out that the monopolisation process is accelerating faster than ever.

A wage cap is essential if we aim to restore a more competitive top flight. But that's not to say that our biggest and wealthiest clubs should be allowed to fade into relative obscurity. Millions of overseas fans support our "big six" teams, and therefore it's important, to some extent, that they continue to perform well. This is because English football's position as a dominant worldwide brand in part depends upon a few glamourous clubs being widely admired by millions of adoring fans. Consequently, there is an added layer of nuance to this debate. If say, Manchester City or Liverpool were to get beaten every week by the likes of Hartlepool Town (sorry Jeff), then this would diminish their sense of importance and prestige. As part of its global appeal, English football needs its Goliaths to perform well. And this is why the Designated Player Rule, if implemented correctly, would still offer those bigger clubs a slight spending advantage, but hopefully not one that would guarantee silverware each season. It's about developing a system which gives Goliath the chance to flex his muscles and sharpen his sword, whilst also ensuring that David keeps some lethal stones in his slingshot.

Essentially, we need to reorientate our approach with regards to implementing future legislation. Instead of focusing on *who* wins the league, we should really concern ourselves with *how many points* wins the league. Looking at the monopolisation process from this angle may afford us the opportunity to be bolder and more experimental with our legislative measures. If we can develop a Premier League competition whereby 70 points generally wins it and 45 points sees you relegated, then we'll really be on to something special. With two games left, everything would still be to play for: five teams in the title race, eight sides vying for European places, and six or seven fearing the drop. Imagine the final day of that season.

The Local Lads

There is another piece of potential legislation that would not only help to reduce wage bills and encourage greater competitiveness but would also be of central importance in supporting our final core principle — promoting local talent. Once again, the MLS model provides some inspiration. In the US, regulation states that every team's squad size should be limited to 30 players. Furthermore, seven of those 30 players must be under the age of 24, and two of them need to have come through the club's academy. Clearly, the MLS is attempting to encourage home-grown talent and youth by keeping squad sizes small and insisting almost one-quarter of the players are under a certain age. So how could we apply these values to our own theoretical model?

In order to promote local talent, a piece of written legislation should insist on clubs doing just that. Under a "Home-Grown Rule", as a point of principle, every team in the top five divisions of the English football pyramid would *have* to field at least two players from the local area who are under the age of 24. This law would apply at all times, so if a player who fell into this category was substituted, then he would need to be replaced by another who also met the criteria. Not only would this ensure that every first team is directly tethered to its local area, but it would also create endless opportunities for English youth players to develop and blossom at every level. Furthermore, it would reduce the possibility of one club winning the title year after year, as a constant conveyor belt of exceptionally gifted youth players would be required to achieve that. Academies would become even more vital to on-field success, because if a club fails to produce youth players of a certain standard, then their first team would have definite weaknesses.

Once again, this is a fluid concept, as it could be lowered to one player, or upped to three, etc. Perhaps when English teams are competing in European cup competitions, it could be abandoned altogether. But, in writing such legislation, the system would be making clubs earn their success, as opposed to buying it. Clubs would need to look inwards as well as outwards because developing quality youth players would be just as important as attracting world-class international talent. Our leagues would preside over a more level playing field, and victories would be sweetened by local lads performing on the pitch. Naturally, clubs would try to cheat the system (as they've always done), therefore the rulebook should be very clear about what "local" entails. The country would be divided into distinct regions (many of which would overlap due to certain clubs' close proximity to one another) so every club knew the exact geographical boundaries of their scouting grounds. There would also need to be regulation which prevented clubs from simply rehousing talented kids from around the country and into their catchment areas. Perhaps a player must have lived there for a certain amount of time in order to meet the residential qualifying criteria? Once again, the details would need to be thrashed out, but the principle is secure. No doubt bigger clubs would still sign exceptionally talented youth prospects, but they wouldn't necessarily qualify as "local" academy players.

The final piece of MLS regulation we should utilise is a limit on first team squad size. This would ensure a more level playing field and tilt the balance back in favour of fair competition. A limited number of first team squad players would also deepen every club's reliance on its own academy, and therefore create more opportunities for local lads to be involved in first team action. If a limit on the number of first team players was imposed, then every team would be bound by the same restrictions, and the richest clubs would be prevented from hoovering up all the playing talent. Throughout the course of a season, key players will always pick up injuries, but a club's riches would not allow them to bring in extra signings via the transfer market. Instead, home-grown academy players would be elevated into the senior team in order to plug any gaps. Allowing teams to grow super-sized squads should not be permitted. A limit on first team squad size provides yet more control and works against the constant threat of monopolisation.

Agents

Creating profit requires a complete reversal of neoliberal practice. Let's be brutally honest, the current system is full of greedy hangers-on with their hands firmly planted in the till, and they need cutting loose. These so-called "super agents" should not be calling the shots — football needs to assert some authority over these reckless profiteers. They seek to aggressively drive wages to ridiculous levels and subsequently take huge percentages from deals. Unbelievably, in the 12-month period between the start of February 2019 and the end of January 2020, agents extracted £263 million from Premier League-based transfers.[2] How could anyone argue that this is part of an effective business model?

A large portion of football's finances remain undisclosed, and therefore agent's fees are likely to be substantially higher than the figure above. This circumstance encapsulates the reality of neoliberalism in a nutshell: individuals extracting wealth from a system whose opaque financial structures encourage nepotism and corruption. It's nothing short of a scandal. Yet we've learned to accept this methodology as a natural part of proceedings, with no template for a competing model currently in place.

Wealthy businessmen have seized upon football's deregulated and globalised marketplace in order to enrich themselves yet further. According to *Forbes*, Jonathan Barnett, one of the UK's most prominent football agents, has taken $128 million (£100 million) from the game in commissions throughout his career.[3] Why are we putting up with this? Player transfers are often complex transactions, but agents surely shouldn't be taking a cumulative £263 million from these transactions each season.

Once again, a lack of protective regulation is undermining the beautiful game. The act of becoming a football agent is incredibly easy to achieve. One must simply head to the FA website, fill in a quick form and then hand over the £500 registration fee. Hey presto, you're now a "fully qualified" football agent. However, if you were to follow this process and (very easily) qualify as an agent, you may quickly discover that finding work becomes close to impossible. Being an agent is all about *who* you know, not what you know. It's often the friends or family members of managers, players or club owners that are given permission to navigate the murky waters of the football transfer system, and obviously pocket some eye-watering sums in the process.

This toxic and unregulated landscape is certainly bad for the game, but it can also prove harmful to players as well. Harry Kane's brother secured him a renewed, six-year deal at Spurs — but with no buy-out clause. When Manchester City came calling, Kane couldn't leave the club, even if he wanted to. He'd been equally let down by an under-qualified member of his own family and a failed system that allows untrained amateurs to draw up multi-million-pound deals. It's ridiculous that any

Tom, Dick or Harry can assume a role as an agent without any appropriate qualifications or safeguarding checks. The system is a racket, and a part of the reason why English football clubs are operating at a financial loss. Even many hardline neoliberals agree. As Alan Sugar once said: "The money coming into the game is incredible, but it is just a prune juice effect, it comes in and goes out straight away. Agents run the game."[4]

Perhaps, Alan, you should have pointed your finger at them and stated those two famous words — "systemic change". If one is to run a football club at a profit, then agents (in their current guise) become a serious problem. A change in ideology is required, and nothing less shall suffice. It's imperative that we begin to think differently and build an entirely new system of governance that serves only the interests of the game. Re-evaluating the role of agents would play a key role in this development. It's time for a rethink. Is it not sensible to suggest that football agents should be trained and regulated? Under this assumption, three basic actions would serve to produce a solid foundation for a new approach designed to combat agent profiteering:

1. Pay agents an annual salary via a centralised regulatory body.
2. Implement a fit and proper persons test with an accompanying training scheme.
3. Scrap the system which facilitates agents receiving transaction and contractual fees.

Under a new system based on these principles, all football agents operating in England would be employed directly by the wider "EF" PCP and paid an annual wage. Their salaries and training schemes could be funded by a tiny percentage of each transfer deal — just a 1% levy would yield tens of millions annually, and thereby provide more than enough capital to pay the wages of a strong agent network. Unlike the untrained amateurs of today, a rigorous training scheme would ensure that all agents under this model are proficient and able to represent their clients properly. An appealing annual salary would provide the sector with competent professionals and all agents would personally receive 0% in commissions from every deal they were involved with.

Could deals be potentially standardised or at least made less bespoke by regulation that simplified the transfer market? This would help reduce the influence of agents and make transfer deals less complex and easier for clubs to get over the line. The modern game can rely on vast amounts of scientific data as every player's movement is tracked and their athleticism reviewed in detail. This provides huge advantages in assessing a player's worth and the opinion of an agent should not be relevant. Clearly, the current situation cannot be allowed to continue because the actions of agents are costing football a fortune. The power of modern agents is illusionary but the amount of money they're sucking out of the game is very much real. What is their actual skill set and how on earth can they justify earning millions of pounds a year? Sweeping systemic change is needed. Yes, players will always require effective representation, however this can be achieved by a well-trained pool of professionals on relatively modest annual salaries.

The Benefits of Limitation

This proposed regulation is not about creating needless red tape and bureaucracy, on the contrary, it's about installing effective management of the footballing landscape. An unplanned "free market" approach to football's finances leads to rather predictable football results. Whereas a well-planned footballing economy would result in more competitive, less predictable and by extension more exciting football. Both on and off the pitch, new rules have always been introduced into the beautiful game for its betterment. Football improved massively when the offside rule came into being because it created a far more interesting spectacle and added a new dimension to the game. Instead of just constantly dribbling with the ball, players started passing more as teamwork became integral and complex tactical formations began to evolve. In football, rules that reduce individualism and promote collectivism are essential — the Victorians knew this all too well.

Football is still evolving, and the recent emergence of new rules and new technologies is proof of this continuous development. True, new regulations are always a good idea when they improve football as a form of entertainment. Usually, these new rules are preventative, as in they stop players, teams or clubs from doing something. As is so often the case with sport (and also business), limiting what can be done leads to a flurry of innovation. Who could argue that the back-pass rule introduced in the early 1990s was a mistake? Preventing goalkeepers from picking up the ball via a back pass has improved the game no end by reducing time-wasting and giving strikers a bigger advantage. What about the ban on tackling from behind? That rule protects skilful ball carriers and allows for a more entertaining version of football. All these rules were contentious at the time of their introduction but very quickly became regarded as common-sense practice. However, the jury is still out on the use of Video Assistant Referees (VAR), perhaps because they're not actually preventing anything. Instead, this intervention slows the game down and upsets the moment. The real irony is that VAR was created in an attempt to make football fairer whilst an unchallenged monopolisation process serves to work against that principle entirely.

Off the pitch, any new regulation must promote sporting integrity and fair competition, because this is precisely what has been lacking in the modern era. By imposing limits on spending and squad size, we're not hampering football — we're freeing it from the constraints of neoliberalism's predictable and soulless outcomes. Undoubtedly, a more competitive Premier League would provide better entertainment and football's history books are clear on what piece of regulation is needed to achieve this.

Reinstalling a salary cap is not about looking back into football's past with misty-eyed nostalgia. The previous system was far from perfect. In the post-war period, professional football players were being drastically underpaid by our clubs, demonstrating that a cap can be restrictive in two directions: curtailing excess, and undermining what's owed. A lot of things were wrong with the previous salary cap, and the switch to free market principles did provide English football with a vast array of world-class playing talent. However, over time, free markets have destabilised the financial landscape, and created a less competitive league.

We cannot afford to let the situation deteriorate any longer.

Instead, we must look forward into the future and take with us the concepts that suit us best. A wage cap is perhaps still a controversial idea in England. Implementing one would most likely cause severe discontent amongst the Premier League's most powerful teams, with an enforced limit on wage volume reducing their spending power advantage. No doubt, it would certainly upset the applecart. However, the advantages of controlling the market are so huge, that introducing a salary cap becomes the only common-sense option available. Not only would such a policy enhance the competitiveness of our top leagues, but it affords us the opportunity to put an exact cost on the price of football. Controlling how much clubs spend on wages means that they can be funded accordingly via a central source. As a result, the financial system creates surplus profits that cannot be spent on playing staff. Therefore, clubs would put solid financial plans in place for the future and spend the rest of their profits off the pitch — thus creating a new public service. In this context, the benefits of controlling the market would be felt most acutely by us and the communities we live in.

The real question is not if, but to what extent we should intervene in the market. A wage cap and its supporting legislation can be whatever we want it to be, so its limitations would be defined by our predetermined ethical objectives, and these may change over time. We just need to be brave enough to start the experiment. In time, our matured, well-cultivated set of regulations would work to provide financial stability to an environment which has been otherwise chaotic and facilitate an appropriate level of unpredictability to our league competitions. If we can begin to do this, then finding that elusive balance between attracting world class players, creating profit, promoting local talent, and ensuring fair competition, may not be as difficult as we first imagined.

Creating a New Public Service

If we command our wealth, we shall be rich and free; if our wealth commands us, we are poor indeed.
                    Edmund Burke, *Letters on a Regicide Peace*

Under the stewardship of collective ownership, our football clubs would be funded completely differently to how they are now. The profits produced by the likes of the oil industry or billionaire hedge funds would have no place in our national sport. Advertising would once again be banned, along with private investment and its authoritarian rule. Instead, football would be fully democratised and funded collectively by millions of fans paying into an affordable subscription programme. Controlling the financial landscape in a responsible manner would consign football debt to the history books, as clubs become profitable enterprises, serving the wants and needs of their local communities.

A club's balance sheet would have the majority of its outgoings covered by a central funding source, and have its own independent commercial strategies in place. As annual funding from "EF" would cover player wages and general operating costs, membership payments, gate receipts, player sales and merchandise sales would all generate profit. A wage cap would control how much is allowed to be spent on players, however the Designated Player Rule would offer clubs a little freedom to invest heavily in elite talent. Therefore, in order to mitigate against overspending, strict regulation would insist that only 25% of a club's independent commercial income would be available to spend on playing staff. Such a measure helps insulate every club from debt.

Those who finance football hold sway over its governance. If the following theoretical model was to be adopted, the vast majority of English football's funding would come directly from the bank accounts of overseas subscribers paying to watch Premier League action. Consequently, the wants and wishes of those who make up PLTV's international subscriber base would be of great importance. We must ask ourselves, *why* do approximately 200 hundred million people around the world pay to watch Premier League football and how do we retain their custom? Ensuring these people part with £10 a month to watch our football becomes a main priority.

Undoubtedly, Murdoch's rebranding of the English top flight has delivered huge commercial success. The Premier League is now arguably the most popular league in world football and this circumstance creates a huge opportunity for us to enrich ourselves and our communities. Therefore, its position as a global brand is of central importance to EF's business model. As the saying goes, "if it ain't broke, don't fix it". The Premier League body is definitely doing something right in attracting so many customers, so we do need to strike the right balance with future reforms and make sure we are not trashing our goldmine. In a globalised world, English football is competing with many other domestic leagues across the planet for the attention (and money) of the beautiful game's followers, therefore its position in the hierarchy should not be taken for granted. True, our fast-flowing style of football will always provide quality entertainment and our much-revered clubs will always provide English football with a certain degree of glamour and prestige. However, is it not practical to suppose that a certain amount of world-class talent plying their trade in England is essential if we are to retain the 200 million customers currently paying to watch our top division? It would be risky to assume otherwise. If, for example, La Liga was to concentrate a huge amount of the world's best players into its domestic setup, then international viewers may subscribe to that league instead. What about the ludicrous spending sprees being adopted by state-owned clubs in Saudi Arabia? The Premier League cannot afford to presume its subscribers would remain loyal should the playing standard diminish in comparison to other leagues. Yes, the Designated Player Rule would play a key role in the acquisition of elite talent, however this measure alone cannot guarantee the Premier League's position as the most glamorous in world football. Therefore, a low-risk strategy would exist to keep Premier League wage bills very high in order to ensure world-class talent is ever-present and therefore sustain PLTV as an attractive proposition to international customers.

But if we are to host the best league in world football, then how much would the wage bill cost? This question compels us to focus on the finances of other leagues in football's richest continent. A wage cap would need to consider the salaries paid in other European leagues in order to be effective in attracting a high standard of players. So what does this wider economic landscape reveal? As it stands, English football's top tier is easily outspending every other league on the planet on wages. During the 2020/21 season (the latest figures available at the time of writing), the annual median salary for top-flight players in England, Spain, Italy, Germany and France was as follows:

Premier League = £2.9 million
La Liga = £2 million
Serie A = £1.6 million
Bundesliga = £2.4 million
Ligue 1 = £1 million[1]

As we can see, the Premier League could afford to reduce its median player salary by one-third and *still* match its nearest spending competitor, the Spanish La Liga. At the very least, these statistics reveal a little wriggle room for downward pressure on salaries. However, that's not to say that we should necessarily look to decrease wage bills in the short term (although that may become a long-term objective). As mentioned before, a low-risk strategy would initially seek to protect wages in order to maintain a high number of quality players and reinforce the Premier League's position as a dominant worldwide brand. However, focusing purely on a league's median salary would prove to be a mistake. This is because the monopolisation process is even more extreme on the continent, with a small host of super clubs drastically outspending their domestic competitors. Therefore, if English clubs are to remain competitive in the European Champions League, then it's vital to consider the wage bills of these domineering giants. Because clubs aren't in a hurry to publish their accounts, the most up-to-date figures are difficult to come by, so I liaised with Kieran Maguire (one of football's leading financial experts and author of *The Price of Football*) in order to ascertain how much money elite clubs are currently spending on playing staff. According to his estimations, it ranges between £300–£400 million a season. Recent history suggests that this ballpark figure will likely rise in the coming seasons.

Moreover, because English football is now in direct competition with Saudi Arabia for the signatures of world-class talent, it would be sensible to slash tax rates for players in our top division. With the oil industry injecting such huge amounts of cash into the worldwide transfer market, our hand is being forced. Therefore, footballers plying their trade in the Premier League would only pay 1% tax. This initiative is a safeguard, ensuring that the PL continues to attract the interest of global stars. If need be, the proposed 1% threshold could be reduced. This is because world-class players are an essential part of the Premier League subscription package, and the amount of money entering their bank accounts is of great concern to them, and therefore us. The potential profits garnered through 200 million or so monthly subscribers would render such a tax break insignificant — an annual kitty of £24 billion is definitely worth protecting.

But before we delve into any hypothetical distribution models, there are three pieces of theoretical regulation to implement. These rules are designed to simplify the financial landscape, encourage fair competition and provide consistency throughout the leagues. First and foremost is the previously referenced salary cap on overall squad expenditure, accompanied by the Designated Player Rule:

A limit on squad wage bills and transfer fees would be applied, with clubs permitted to spend up to 25% of their own commercial profits on three additional players.

Secondly, in a rule that would be applied across the top five tiers of the English pyramid:

> Every first team squad would be limited to 33 players — 30 inside the wage cap and three under the Designated Player Rule.

Finally, this piece of legislation would apply throughout the first 10 tiers of the English footballing pyramid:

> Every league, whether regional or national, will consist of 20 teams.

So under these guidelines, how could the riches produced by the world's most popular sport be better circulated?

The Premier League

Clearly, English football's cash cow must be protected by high player wages and therefore the average median salary has been raised.[2] Player contracts would still be bespoke, with some players earning far more than others, although a median group salary level offers a general guideline for clubs to follow. EF would fund each Premier League outfit with:

- A £200 million payment to cover total wage expenditure = 30 players on a median salary of £6.6 million a season.
- An additional £75 million transfer kitty.

Therefore, all Premier League teams would receive a combined total of £275 million in order to level the financial playing field. However, with 25% of a club's independent commercial gains available to spend on three additional players, this would allow some clubs to keep pace with the £400 million a season currently being spent by Europe's top clubs. Overall cost of funding the Premier League = **£5.5 billion**

Tiers Two–Five

Once again, player contracts would be bespoke, with a median salary offering only a guideline. Promotion and relegation rules would be uniform with three up and three down across all leagues (the third promotion spot decided by the age-old tradition of play-offs). All five leagues would remain national and the divisions below the Premier league would be renamed for the purposes of logic and chronology. The Championship would be called "League 2" and the third tier "League 3" and so on.

Our second tier would also need to be well-funded as it's the gateway to the best league on the planet, so the quality of players needs to be of a high standard. The wage cap would present a sliding scale as we go down the pyramid, but overall wages should be upped and the profession of being a footballer fully respected. It takes an incredible amount of skill, sacrifice and dedication to become a professional footballer, and an improved financial distribution system would open the door to better terms of pay for those that make the grade. Instead of talking about the "92" professional league clubs, we would be referencing the "100" instead as an extra division is incorporated into this group. Every club would be well-funded. However, as with the Premier League, clubs are expected to manage their own finances independently.

League 2
- 45 million per club for wages = 30 players on a median annual salary of £1.5 million.
- £30 million transfer kitty.
  Total cost of League 2 = **£1.5 billion**

League 3
- £18 million per club for wages = 30 players on a median annual salary of £600,000.
- £7 million transfer kitty
  Total cost of League 3 = **£500 million**

League 4
- £9 million per club for wages = 30 players on a median annual salary of £300,000.
- £6 million transfer kitty
  Total cost of League 4 = **£300 million**

League 5
- £6 million for wages = 30 players on a median annual salary of £200,000.
- £4 million transfer kitty
  Total cost of League 5 = **£200 million**

Regulating the transfer market in this manner presents two major benefits. Firstly, it creates space for clubs to become profitable. As a central source would be funding the vast majority of outgoings, a club's independent commercial revenue would become profit. Furthermore, a club doesn't necessarily *have* to spend the maximum amount allotted for player wages or transfer fees, it could choose to spend less and increase profits further. Secondly, the premium wages on offer would ensure a high standard of football throughout the entire pyramid. Not only would Premier League clubs be able to afford the most exciting players in world football, but our lower divisions would attract a higher calibre of talented playing staff. For perspective, the League 2 median salary would be at a similar level to that of Serie A and higher than France's Ligue 1.

Upping wages in the lower tiers of the English pyramid would have a knock-on effect which threatened a core EF principle. So another piece of protective legislation is required. It's highly probable that players from all over the world would seek to sign contracts in our third, fourth and fifth divisions, and, as a result, local talent may be overlooked. Therefore, the "Home-Grown Rule" would need to be stricter in the lower leagues in order to ensure that our clubs fielded teams which were representative of their local communities. Wage bills may represent a sliding scale as we go down the leagues, but the Home-Grown Rule would work in the opposite direction:

The Home-Grown Rule:
Premier League = 2 players
League 2 = 2 players
League 3 = 3 players
League 4 = 4 players
League 5 = 4 players

In order to protect British football players and simultaneously prevent other domestic leagues from being hollowed out, there would also need to be a limit on the number of overseas players fielded in lower divisions. From the fourth tier down, clubs would be allowed to field a maximum of three non-British players on the pitch. Moving up the pyramid, this rule would be relaxed in the third tier to four players and abandoned altogether in the top two divisions to ensure the highest standard of football possible.

Obviously, there are huge discrepancies between the wage bills of different tiers, and this could result in relegated teams struggling to meet the guidelines imposed by their new league. In order to address this, all professional contracts in England would require a blanket legal term which automatically decreases the annual salary of a player should their team be relegated. Accordingly, if a team were to be promoted, then the salaries of the playing staff who achieved it would all increase. Such a measure would help further control the transfer market and ensure that relegation was never a financial burden to any club.

Egalitarian Economics

To best serve the interests of its members and wider society, and guarantee disposable income, English Football's new public service would have another fiscal gift up its sleeve for the top 100. At an overall cost of £500 million, all clubs in the top five divisions of the English pyramid would receive an additional annual payment of £5 million each. This payment would come with one simple condition — it cannot be spent on upgrading playing squads, coaching staff or managers. This annual imbursement is designed to be spent off the pitch, flooding money into our communities through schemes, social projects or business development opportunities. In a complete devolution of economic power, naturally it would be up to members to democratically decide what to do with the money allocated to their club. With £5 million a year guaranteed, regardless of which division a club is in, long-term investment plans and ambitious projects could be undertaken that suit the needs and wants of local areas. Such a scheme would give overused phrases such as "levelling-up" and "trickle-down economics" some genuine gravitas and begin to establish football as an egalitarian social platform.

Total overall cost of funding the top five tiers of English professional football = **£8.5 billion**

The Academy Cup

As well as restructuring the league format, the EFL Cup would also be subject to change. In this model, an overload of games increases the likelihood of burnout and injury because first team squads are limited to 33 players. Therefore, it makes sense to lessen the burden and reduce an over-congested fixture list, particularly for teams competing in European competitions. So the EFL Cup would become the Academy Cup. This switch would insist that all teams competing in England's second most prestigious cup competition field players under the age of 23. There are a number of benefits to this format. Firstly, it protects first team squads from injury by lessening their game time. Secondly, it would provide academy teams with the opportunity to perform in the national spotlight and for a few games a season actually replace the first team entirely. Thirdly, it nudges English football's cultural focus away from globalisation and back towards locality and youth development.

Critics of an Academy Cup would likely point out that such a measure would diminish the importance of the competition, as the majority of first team players wouldn't be performing. However, isn't this already the case for many Premier League teams? In recent years, many managers have been criticised for treating the EFL Cup as an experimental exercise in squad rotation, particularly so in the earlier rounds. However, that hasn't stopped the biggest spenders from totally dominating the competition (no teams outside the traditional "big six" have claimed the trophy in the last decade). Therefore it makes sense to level the playing field and allow every club to experiment as future stars are effectively elevated to first team status. This change would also result in the FA Cup regaining some of its former prestige. In the modern era, commentators regularly talk about the "magic of the FA Cup". Previously, this phrase wasn't used in relation to football's longest running competition because it didn't need to be. The glamour of the FA Cup has been overshadowed by the rise of the Champions League and its "magic" has been somewhat diminished. In restoring its former position as the only first team cup competition, at the very least, a little more of that magic would return.

Tiers Six–Ten

As mentioned earlier, every division throughout tiers 6–10 would be numerically identical and contain 20 teams each. Geographically mirroring the current format, from here on in, all leagues would become regional. Football's central source would fund the wage bill of every competing club and also provide additional income to help with operating costs, infrastructure development and academy expansion. Once again, individual clubs (or rather their collective members) would be trusted to spend the money however they saw fit.

Below the fifth tier, wage regulation would become increasingly strict. To promote fair competition, every squad would be limited to 30 players, all of whom would be purchased within the limitations of a wage cap. The Designated Player Rule would be abolished altogether, and the Home-Grown Rule would be extended to five players across the board.

Under this new economic framework, professional football would be expanded further down the pyramid, creating thousands of full-time playing contracts. Wages would be upped considerably, and it would be possible to earn a decent living playing as far down as the ninth tier. Enabling players to play and train full-time would lift the standard of football and create thousands of extra jobs in the football industry, thus benefiting the wider economy. From players and coaching teams to catering staff and admin roles, football clubs at this level would be responsible for hiring hundreds of employees in their local communities.

Tier Six

As it does now, the sixth tier would include two divisions — north and south — which run parallel to one another. As these two regional leagues would feed a singular national fifth tier, the promotion procedure becomes slightly more complex. The winners of both the northern and southern divisions would gain automatic promotion into League 5 and the runners up would enter a play-off final to decide the third spot. This showpiece final would become one of the most important games in English football, with the victors guaranteed a bonus of £5 million to spend on their communities the following season.

The 40 clubs in tier six would all receive funding of £8 million each which would be divided into:

- £2 million for player wages = median salary of £66,666.
- £6 million for general operating costs, transfer fees and community projects.
  Total cost of tier six = **£320 million**

Tier Seven
This would comprise 80 teams across four regional divisions. Each club would receive funding of £5 million each:

- £1.5 million for player wages = median salary of £50,000.
- £3.5 million for general operating costs, transfer fees and community projects.
  Total cost of tier seven = **£400 million**

Tier Eight
This would include 160 clubs playing across eight regional divisions. At this level, all playing contracts would become identical and match the median salary offered. Each club would receive £4 million a season:

- £1.2 million for player wages = 30 contracts worth £40,000 per annum.
- £2.8 million for general operating costs, transfer fees and community projects.
  Total cost of tier eight = **£640 million**

Tier Nine
Made up of 320 teams spanning 16 different regions, all player contracts would be identical and match the median salary offered. Each club would receive £2.5 million:

- £750,000 for player wages = 30 contracts all worth £25,000 per annum.
- £1.75 million for general operating costs, transfer fees and community projects.
  Total cost of tier nine = **£800 million**

Tier Ten

Tier Ten currently comprises 335 teams, however, with the new model insisting on a uniform 20 teams in each division, that figure would be upped to 340 clubs. Each club would receive £1 million in funding and players would be offered a standardised semi-professional contract:

- £360,000 for player wages = 30 contracts worth £12,000 per annum.
- £640,000 for general operating costs, transfer fees and community projects.
  Total cost of tier ten = **£340 million**

Total cost of funding tiers six to ten = £2.5 billion

Therefore, the cost of funding the top ten tiers of professional football equates to £11 billion. All clubs would be profitable and financial decision-making would be made at the local level by members and their democratically elected club officials. All the while, effective financial regulation would ensure fair competition on the pitch whilst a written constitution would provide a framework for governing bodies.

Education

Through an annual outlay of £500 million, the public service of football would be integrated with our education sector. Similar to the approach taken by the NFL, a set education programme could be woven into every professional and semi-professional player's developmental stage. An extensive scheme would provide all prospective players with coaching and teaching skills throughout their progression. Because the vast majority of academy players do not end up earning a living out of playing professional football, it makes sense to provide all young promising talent with regular educational courses — meaning they have a fall-back position and a wide range of transferable skills to apply in the wider economy.

With professional football being expanded further down the pyramid, there would also be a huge increase in full-time playing staff. As part of their professional contracts, those working as professionals in the lower tiers of the pyramid would be obliged to visit schools and teach physical education on a regular basis. All academy players above the age of 16 would be undertaking similar roles as they gain qualifications and progress through the educational scheme. To the benefit of our schools and communities, tens of thousands of sports coaches would be trained, paid and fully supported by the service of football.

The idea here is simple: an expanded football sector could provide schools with capable, well-trained professional and semi-professional athletes who would teach physical education (or coach football) to pupils. Offering this service to schools free of charge would provide a number of tangible benefits. From a school's perspective, it would ease financial budgets and take pressure away from overburdened teaching staff. From a child's perspective, it would give all pupils the opportunity to be taught by professional athletes, thus providing inspiration, raising self-esteem and giving them a richer educational experience. Moreover, interlocking football clubs with schools and the wider national curriculum would improve the level of coaching and raise the overall standard of football in this country. It would also create a more meaningful link between club and community, not to mention the potential scouting opportunities on offer for clubs.

Funding the FA

Presently, the FA relies on financial assistance from a wide range of commercial partners, such as Barclays, M&S Food and Nuffield Health. According to their website, during the 2021/22 season, the FA invested £119 million into the English game, funding coaching programmes, disability football, facilities, prize money, player welfare, referees and women's football.

Instead, an annual kitty of £250 million would be allocated to the FA so that they can rid themselves of commercial partners and massively expand their capabilities, thus providing a better service to the people of our nation. One of the key drivers should be to up participation in football across all age-groups, as this would provide tangible health benefits to the nation as a whole whilst improving general well-being and happiness.

Funding Women's Football

The women's game has grown significantly in recent years. According to Deloitte, the aggregate revenue for the 12 WSL clubs reached £32 million in 2021/2022, up 60% from the previous season.[3] With the success of the Lionesses in the UEFA Women's Euros, attendances in the WSL increased significantly. Undoubtedly, the popularity of women's football in England is on an upward trajectory. However, the women's game seems to be repeating the mistakes of the men's game in the sense that there are huge discrepancies in wage bills and a process of hyper-commercialisation is well under way.

Instead, women's football should be structured in a manner that upholds fair competition at the elite level, eradicates intrusive sponsorship deals and ensures democratic procedures. Additionally, in order to attract bigger audiences and establish itself as a worldwide brand, our domestic Women's Super League should play host to a large share of world class players. All of this can be achieved by introducing a salary cap (with a Designated Player Rule), eradicating sponsorship, democratising ownership of clubs and upping player wages.

The women's game would receive an annual bursary of £250 million. This would ensure high wages throughout the footballing pyramid, thousands of full-time professional contracts, improved infrastructure and enough money for collectively owned clubs to provide for their local communities. Membership payments would replicate that of the men's game and be incorporated into the wider PCP that represents the English football industry. Furthermore, all female professional and semi-professional players would be included in the players' educational scheme, thus increasing the number of qualified coaches and providing a wide range of wider vocational skills.

A more thorough analysis of the future of women's football is a book in itself, therefore only the most basic overview is offered here. One could rightfully argue that a funding figure of £250 million is far too low in comparison to the men's game. However, a figure of £250 million raises the current revenue for the women's game by over 800%, which is still a significant increase. True, this rather vague model provides more questions than answers. What percentage of Premier League riches should be allocated to women's football? How should the game be governed? These are wider political debates that this book cannot pursue. But one thing is certain, the women's game needs to grow and establish its own unique culture and identity. In order for that process to mature at a faster pace, it requires more funding than is currently allocated. Moreover, if the riches produced by the Premier League are to fund football as a public service, then the women's game most definitely needs to be incorporated.

The above model highlights what could be achieved with £12 billion, a figure that is at the lower end of how much money a reimagined footballing industry could potentially administer. In fact, considering the revenue produced by Premier League broadcasting on a worldwide scale, this amount of money is already being generated by English football. Indeed, £25 billion would not be a fantastical figure to be playing with, just imagine what could be achieved with that? Under the reign of market fundamentalism, football's riches can only be concentrated at the top. It's time to create an economic system which is capable of commanding wealth more effectively.

Levelling Up

Firstly, it is about empowering local leaders and local communities and reversing centralisation...

Neil O'Brien, Parliamentary Under-Secretary of
State at the Department for Levelling Up,
Housing and Communities

As discussed previously, if we were to assume collective ownership of English football, then we could manufacture and export our product directly to the rest of the world. Consequently, with effective regulation, a tightly controlled market and a well-planned footballing economy, billions of pounds would become available for us to spend however we saw fit. This circumstance would allow us to do what successive governments have failed to — invest properly in people through education, skills, training programmes and community projects. For the previous 40 years, the urge to marketise every aspect of the way we live has gifted ever-increasing amounts of control to unelected financial elites. This process has transferred huge amounts of money from the public to the private sphere, often enriching those already at the top end of the fiscal food chain. As a result, public services are being downgraded, levels of inequality are stark and our weakened, over-financialised economy is unable to cope with wider shocks. Consequently, the standard of living for millions of people in Britain is being reduced.

Amidst a cut-throat economy of haves and have-nots, the public service of football should aim to reverse these trends, thus stitching the fabric of our society back together and generating wealth for public good. Virtually every club would likely use the profits produced by a cunningly reformatted manufacturing sector to invest properly in human capital, building tighter-knit, more prosperous communities and promoting social cohesion.

If funded appropriately, collectively owned football clubs harbour the potential to boost the UK's stagnant economy. A modern football club is a multifaceted organisation that extends way beyond the pitch, comprising of various businesses interconnected under a unified umbrella. This encompasses retail shops, bars, restaurants, entertainment spaces, hotels, marketing agencies, multiple charities, community outreach initiatives and so much more. These businesses all have the potential to deepen their social responsibilities, not just creating more jobs, but also improving well-being and general happiness. Our football clubs are already the beating heart of our communities, so why not give them a more central role in our local economies? There are ample opportunities for profitable footballing Public-Common Partnerships to influence other sectors of the wider marketplace, creating healthy competition in both the public and private spheres. The idea is to break traditional monopolies, undermine centralised power structures, give greater autonomy to local regions, promote democratic procedure and offer people control and ownership of their own services. Democratising football isn't about people casting a vote every four years and watching events unfold from the sidelines. Rather, it's about providing communities with independence and allowing groups of people to come together and figure things out for themselves.

In a calculated bid to combat the humiliating effects of centralised power, the service of football should practise the "rule of subsidiary" — meaning all decision-making is pushed down to the lowest level possible. Following the rule of subsidiary whenever feasible would ensure that local people have a proper say in how their club spends money in their community, town or city. The implementation of this rule would make it virtually impossible to accurately predict how money might be spent, because every membership base would have complete autonomy over its own club's spending plans. Members may innovate as new ways of spending money for public good are imagined. Therefore, the following ideas are merely suggestive, offering only a possible blueprint for how the football sector could operate as a public service. Although every region of England has its own unique challenges and cultural quirks, there are also many problems and challenges that we commonly share. So here are just a few ideas of how millions of pounds may be invested.

Upgrading Stadium Infrastructure
Surely, this measure would be undertaken by every club. Our football stadiums are not just iconic, they're almost holy ground for many supporters, providing a sense of belonging and pride in one's locality. Extra seating capacity would certainly be needed if matchday ticket prices were affordable (or free) to the masses, but a football club offering public services to its members would need to diversify and expand its capabilities off the pitch. Under a model of collectivised ownership, our stadiums would become common ground for members to enjoy (as opposed to private spaces fenced off from the public). Events spaces and other commercial enterprises would be incorporated into or built alongside

our club's stadiums as members decide upon which services to enact. If football clubs were to become vibrant educational facilities, then spaces to teach, nurture and inspire pupils would need to be created. Moreover, these spaces could be used for different purposes in the evening as meeting places, adult educational settings, sporting facilities or commercial enterprises. What about providing quality entertainment? The point being that our stadiums would be a constant hive of activity, open to the public day and night as they provide for people and community.

Building Multi-Functional Community Centres

If football is to become an effective public service, then our clubs would need to spread their roots deeper into communities. Because Public-Common Partnerships are partly governed by local councils, our football clubs could be granted easy access to land for development. With millions of pounds available in the coffers, football clubs could build a network of multi-use community centres in and around their local areas. These community centres could be used for a variety of purposes, each of which would be decided upon by members. Throughout the working days of the week, these establishments could be used as educational settings, coaching facilities, childcare and nursery services, or perhaps a café for relaxing and socialising. What about a shared gardening or agricultural project? Struggling to get an appointment with your local doctor, then what about a drop-in medical centre? By night, a community centre could transform into an event space or a bar/pub for locals to enjoy cheap drinks and entertainment. What about a large function room so supporters can watch away games together on a big screen? Perhaps a number of charities would operate from the premises. What about offering regular educational courses for adults? From computer coding and needlework classes to vibrant debating conferences, our clubs could be places to better yourself and spaces to engage in wider community events or discussions. The public service of football would aim to expand into our communities with bricks and mortar, bringing us closer together and providing common ground for everyone to enjoy.

Health, Leisure and Entertainment

The health, leisure and entertainment industries all offer further opportunities for the service of football to provide for its collective subscriber base. Going out and enjoying yourself has become a rather costly venture in the 2020s as inflation continues to force everyday prices up. Could the service of football help bring down the financial cost of enjoying our favourite pastimes? Community centres could be used for these purposes, or perhaps your club may want to invest in a separate venue. Working in tandem with a network of publicly owned breweries, our clubs could be serving members with discounted alcoholic drinks, which would certainly tempt a lot of people to join up. If for £11 a month you can acquire cheap drinks and free entertainment at a local venue, then it would surely tempt more people to subscribe to their local club and grow the pot (it wouldn't even matter if they were interested in football or not).

If frequenting bars, restaurants and social clubs doesn't float your boat, then what about fitness training, weightlifting or practising yoga? One good option would be to build multiple gyms around the city or region. Not only would this provide huge health benefits to the local area by allowing more people to access gyms, but it would also mean that members could potentially cancel any costly membership fees they may already be paying to gyms in the private sector. Moreover, investing in a publicly owned network of quality gymnasiums would likely grow our football clubs' membership subscription base. Why pay in the region of £30 a month to go to the gym when you could sign up to your local football club and pay £11?

Financial Lending

If English football's riches were to be distributed effectively throughout our country, then this would create a surplus which could then be spent on economic development. Essentially, through recalibrating certain financial regulations, our football clubs could become public money-lending institutions. Presently, financial lending is at the discretion of private banks, who must always put the interests of private shareholders first. Such a system has hampered economic development in the UK. If you've ever created a business plan and applied for a bank loan without any existing financial assets, then you will likely have been rejected. This is because banks don't like lending money unless they can seek collateral if a loan turns bad. The banking sector is happy to lend people money for a mortgage because if repayments can't be made, the bank can assume ownership of the house. But working-class people trying to improve their lot with a brilliant business plan are often seen as a risky venture. In order to grow our economy in the long-term and raise productivity, we need a financial sector that actively wants to support small and medium-sized businesses as a priority. Essentially, modern Britain needs financial lending institutions which are prepared to prioritise entrepreneurial risk as opposed to shareholder payouts. Our football clubs could migrate into the UK financial sector, acting as collectively owned banking institutions. Football's financial lending model should be kept simple, each club could allocate a certain amount of funding to be used for interest-free business loans. When the money is repaid, it could then be recycled back into the system and loaned out again. A perfect virtuous economic cycle that doesn't involve creating money out of thin air. Therefore, rather than applying to a high street bank for a business loan, members could apply directly to their local football club's financial department — a panel of knowledgeable experts embedded within the local community. Such a scheme would devolve economic power to local regions, offer people more financial lending options and put pressure on central banks to be more competitive.

Billions Not Millions

If our global product was manufactured and delivered to a high enough standard, and regulation controlled player wages effectively, then the profits produced by English football would total tens of billions of pounds a year. This would allow us to be more ambitious with our plans off the pitch. Working alongside local councils and national government, a supporter-owned footballing sector could use these vast sums to upgrade not just our citizens' life chances, but also our country's wider infrastructure.

The following ideas would require subsidies and support from central government. In order to ensure this, we could create an investment partnership between state and Common Association, thus devolving economic and political power to ourselves. In this sense, we could use a collectively owned footballing sector to lobby our own national government, demanding that large investments be made into developing or upgrading regional infrastructure. The inherent short-termism of the neoliberal agenda has failed to invest in long-term projects — we should not repeat this mistake in the future. Moreover, it has created a system whereby most political lobbying takes place in the shadows at the behest of corporate elites, vested interests or wealthy individuals. Instead, we could reverse that trend by using the Common Association as a powerful lobbying tool, thus creating huge amounts of political pressure, widening the public debate and loosening the chains of centralised control.

Transport
Improving local transport networks would take cars off the road, improve air quality, reduce carbon emissions and move people quickly around cities, thus helping the economy thrive. In fact, as one of its overarching directives, the service of football could be focused upon building improved transport links within every region of the country. Football and public transport are inextricably linked; they grew together, side by side, in a symbiotic relationship. Our railway system was once the envy of the entire world, but decades of privatisation and chronic under-investment have left it in a sorry state of disrepair. An archaic and crumbling network, in which commuters pay the highest fares in Europe, has proven to be an embarrassing legacy of neoliberalism's failure to serve the hardworking majority. Why does the sixth richest country in the world only have two cities (London and Newcastle) with an underground tube system? It is a political decision and a failure of successive governments. The service of football could play a role in modernising and improving our transport system, thus providing fandom with a network befitting their loyal support. From fleets of new buses to enhanced rail services, our local transport networks within and between cities could be improved year upon year.

Energy

It's not just our country's stuttering transport network that needs updating. Football as a public service could provide regions with the opportunity to become more resilient to wider economic shocks by creating their own localised energy infrastructures. Football clubs local to each other could pool their resources and build wind farms or other sources of renewable energy. With the recent price hike in energy bills, such an investment would pay for itself over time and enable football clubs to become carbon neutral. Every stadium roof has the potential to be fitted with massive solar panels which could create huge amounts of energy, especially in the summer months. Moreover, surplus energy could be supplied to other local institutions, such as hospitals and schools, or wherever members decide. Our clubs could become energy providers, giving regions greater independence, boosting the wider economy and taking pressure away from the national grid.

Reversing the North/South Divide

In the UK, money and power are being increasingly concentrated in London. Our economy skews towards the southeast as a metropolitan elite preside over an agenda of London-centric policy making. Vacuous slogans such as "Northern powerhouse" or "Midlands engine" are used by the government in an attempt to persuade voters that the regional imbalance will soon be addressed. It's time we took matters into our own hands via a structured devolution of economic power and financial decision-making. The public service of football would aim to distribute revenue far more evenly across the pyramid, and therefore our country as a whole. Because every club would also generate its own independent commercial revenue, some Common Associations (belonging to clubs with worldwide fanbases) would have huge sums of money to play with. In fact, when you consider the economic potential of England's football clubs, a rather interesting reversal of the north-south divide reveals itself. Indeed, it is the north-west region of England that harbours our wealthiest and most globally revered clubs. Consequently, this area of the country stands to benefit hugely from an economic model aiming to capitalise on the global status of our domestic football and reinvest profits directly into local communities and infrastructure. Furthermore, construction costs and land purchases would be far cheaper in northern regions compared to London and the south-east.

For example, when you consider the revenue of the two biggest Manchester clubs, then, economically speaking, it starts to get rather exciting for the region. The Glazers have supposedly extracted over £1 billion from Manchester United alone, evidencing how much money a football club with a global brand can generate. Therefore, two global brands in one city could be focused on investing in the local economy whilst implementing a wide range of schemes, from small community projects to massive infrastructure investments. Both clubs will have access to huge revenue streams via club membership subscriptions, not to mention the redirected finances pouring in from a new public sector model. Regulation which ensured wage bills were funded would allow massive profits to be made, resulting in exciting opportunities for the city. With both clubs enjoying huge international fanbases, the membership payments generated by tens of millions of supporters all around the globe would be eye-watering. Could a two-club city such as Manchester even begin to lobby the national government and push the agenda for an underground transport system to be built? A combination of two very wealthy and influential

Public-Common Partnerships operating in the same city could broker a deal with the national government, demanding the implementation of a long-term investment plan. Over decades, the neoliberal economic agenda has continuously shied away from investing properly in the wider UK economy. An underground tube network in Manchester would reduce pollution, create ease of travel, provide jobs, boost the local economy and give the words "Northern powerhouse" some genuine gravitas. It's worth noting that Merseyside also harbours two of the richest clubs in world football — Liverpool FC and Everton FC. Operating together as well-funded Public-Common Partnerships, both would have the potential to create similar potential infrastructure projects for the city of Liverpool.

Our nation is blessed with an incredible number of historic football clubs which would all invest in upgrading England. Staying in the northwest region, the likes of Burnley FC, Blackburn Rovers, Bolton Wanderers, Wigan Athletic and Blackpool FC, all clubs which have enjoyed stints in the Premier League over recent years, would funnel funds into local communities through the public service of football. What about the network of historic clubs that populate the Midlands? Birmingham City and Aston Villa would pour money into England's second city, with nearby Wolverhampton Wanderers, West Bromwich Albion, Coventry City, Walsall FC, Shrewsbury Town and Stoke City (to name but a few) helping stimulate the wider West Midlands economy. Funds would also be injected into the neighbouring East Midlands region with Nottingham Forest, Notts County, Derby County and Leicester City all in close proximity to one another. On and on we could go, describing a network of clubs spanning the entire nation. Would clusters of local clubs even decide to pool their resources and each contribute funds to wider regional projects? It would be in the interest of clubs connected by geographical proximity to be in constant dialogue with one another as members democratically decide what to do with profits and lobby central government through the Common Association. Every densely populated area in England would have a famous club to rely on, whilst more rural neighbourhoods could benefit from funds received via smaller, local clubs. "Levelling up" indeed — perhaps we could replace the empty rhetoric of careerist neoliberal politicians with a serious economic plan, aiming to devolve financial decision-making to local areas and invest in long-term economic strategies.

Empowering Local People and Restoring Local Pride
Profitable football clubs, operating as Public-Common Partnerships, have the potential to bring communities together and provide a platform for multiple public debates. Perhaps charities would be set up to help the homeless or the elderly? Or would members buy a fleet of electric buses to get people around the city free of charge and ferry fans to matches? What about providing free childcare and after-school clubs in order to help hard-working parents? Who knows? The point being that members would decide which services their club provides for them, and this would be a continuous democratic debate — free from any centralised control and authority. A perfect devolution of economic power to local communities.

Bringing football into the public sector would allow us to spend billions of pounds on "levelling up" the entire country. As consumerism accounts for the main bulk of the UK's GDP (and football is a product we readily consume), would it not make more sense to redirect the profits of our own consumerism back towards ourselves? As previously referenced, this would create a virtuous circle of wealth that benefits us, as opposed to the billionaires. But a national economy cannot be sustained by debt-ridden consumers, it needs a healthy manufacturing sector. This is why investing heavily in the manufacturing processes of our most culturally revered product would help level-up our flailing economy and reduce a worrying trade deficit.

The Tory government's plan to "level up the North" was obviously heavily criticised for lacking any meaningful content. Neil O'Brien, a previous Parliamentary Under-Secretary of State for Levelling Up, Housing and Communities, was interviewed on BBC's *Newsnight* in 2021, where in relation to this criticism, he stated:

> Firstly, it is about empowering local leaders and local communities and reversing centralisation... Secondly, it is about improving the economy and living standards, particularly in places that have been poorer for many years. Third, it is about spreading opportunity and improving public services, particularly where they are weaker and fourthly and finally, it is about restoring local pride.

This perfectly illustrates what football as a service would actually achieve. Perhaps we should thank Neil O'Brien and his press team for this fantastic description. However, the current macroeconomic framework, which encourages the (often foreign) private ownership of public services, cannot deliver on any of the above. Mark my words, his economic plan will not serve the public. The system is rigged in favour of financial elites, and its propaganda machine is in constant overdrive.

Marketisation and inequality have not just impacted football but also our daily lives, creating a lingering sense of paranoia throughout much of the population. As crucial services like health, education and housing adopt market-based structures, being part of society's positive market trends becomes increasingly vital. Those who suffer at the wrong end of the financial pyramid are locked out of society's riches and subject to ever-decreasing living standards. Life expectancy is postcode-dependent. Beyond wealth, inequality also influences people's self-esteem.[1] There is a growing sense of desperation amongst large swathes of society, coupled with a feeling that the situation is unchangeable. People can't see a way out, and when the dice are constantly loaded against you, eventually you stop throwing them. Levelling up shouldn't just be about economic principles, it needs to be aimed at infusing a sense of belief back into the disaffected by providing a level playing field in which anyone, no matter what their socio-economic status, can achieve. The public service of football could help rectify some of the many mistakes made by the neoliberal economic agenda by investing in people through education and training schemes across various industrial, social and cultural sectors. Such schemes would benefit the nation as a whole. High levels of low-skilled workers only hamper economic growth by driving down wages, whereas a high-skilled workforce raises productivity, increases job security and improves overall living standards.

Through football, we can develop an economic system which celebrates what it means to be human. Women and men are social beings, desiring connection and validation from one another. We flourish on the incentive of competition but also recognise the importance of cooperation and local community. Our football clubs provide the perfect platform to express these intrinsic human behaviours, and through them we can create common ground for everyone to enjoy.

In contrast to neoliberal systems of management which involve strict hierarchical structures, governing common land requires community bonding and the constant practise of democratic procedures, which as a result "produces more connected, collaborative and powerful collectives".[2]

It's time to try a different type of politics, one where centralised control is replaced by regional and localised authority. Instead of creating catchy three-word slogans or vacuous soundbites, politicians should be allowing local people to decide how, where and when money is spent in their communities. A ready-made nationwide network of football clubs, operating as independent and sovereign PCPs, would provide the perfect framework for a devolution of economic power. Suffice to say, any governmental action which sought to bring about these changes would certainly be "acting in the public interest".

Part 3

Making the Impossible Possible

Who Are We?

What you think, you become.

Buddha

Any attempt to organise a movement seeking to democratise English football and its related industries must first scrutinise who we are as a collective. What are our shared values and objectives? What forces drive our behaviour? Who have the *people* of the people's game really become? These are important questions. Without some agreement on who we are and what we stand for, there can be no movement large enough to usurp the current status quo.

In the past, things were clearer. Football fans used to be overwhelmingly working-class, but the situation is more complex today. In our post-industrial age, services and financialisation have replaced manufacturing, whilst the gentrification of football has turned it into a more family-friendly and middle-class activity. Add a process of globalisation into the mix and the waters are muddied yet further.

It would be a mistake to fall back into nostalgia or cling to unrealistic ambitions about the power of working-class movements. Instead, we must consider the diversity of political views and cultural backgrounds that constitute modern Britain. However, if the aim is to protect and build on the principles that underpin our footballing heritage, then an effort should be made to understand how it was created in the first place. Looking back to the era of football's beginnings may provide some guidance and help us make better sense of the modern age. Rather fittingly, the Victorian era shares a notable likeness with our own time, as it too experienced a transformative technological revolution that reshaped societal norms and structures.

The Victorians were willing to experiment with new ideas as they boldly engaged in the implementation of vast social projects on a national scale. As James Plunkett argues in *End State*, these "great social reforms" all had a common thread: they began with ethical considerations.[1] Instead of adopting typical market-based solutions (which will always prioritise profit and economic efficiency), the Victorians developed new strategies which "put the market at the service of society, not the other way around".[2] Such an approach led to the development of Rule 34. By infusing ethics into their economic policies, the Victorians forged the foundations of a fairer and more prosperous society. From public sewerage systems to free education, we still benefit from their use of "ethical economics" today. But these colossal changes did not happen without pressure from below. Spearheaded by great reformers, a sense of revolutionary collectivism challenged the status quo. Football itself was reimagined through this era of political activism, as a gentleman's amateur pursuit evolved into the people's game. But this clash of the classes didn't produce a conflict involving victors and losers; on the contrary, football produced a harmonious ecosystem which proved beneficial to all levels of the social hierarchy.

With Victorian high society growing ever more wary about the prospect of potential revolution and moral decline, football proved to be a useful instrument of social control as a paranoid establishment sought to contain the masses outside the workplace. However, football wasn't *just* a form of social control being pushed down from above — it also acted as a vehicle for working-class expression. Our national sport became a public platform for the urbanised majority to generate and showcase their own values, but to do so in a safe, non-threatening sporting environment. In this context, football is, by its very nature, paradoxical, as it serves to free us and control us simultaneously.

The footprint of Victorian society is still a hallmark of our national game today. Because football was codified at the height of the British Empire, its governance provided an opportunity for a range of nineteenth-century aristocratic values to assert themselves. Notions of militaristic imperialism and English superiority were blended with a sense of fair play and gentlemanly conduct — a classic mix of Victorian contradictions.

The Victorian Legacy

The attitudes and sensibilities of football's founders are still influencing the hearts and minds of contemporary English fandom. The Victorian definition of "manliness" has played a key role in shaping fandom's relationship with the beautiful game, subtly moulding our mindsets.[3] Football has often been referred to as a "man's game", and this still impacts the way in which we supporters relate to playing styles. English fandom has traditionally admired footballers who show physical strength and determination, more so than those who display silky skills or fancy flicks. We love to applaud a good, strong tackle, and a player who really "sticks his neck out" is often the first on our imagined team sheet. This sentiment has often revealed itself in the type of players selected for our national team — only in England could Carlton Palmer receive over twice as many international caps as Matt Le Tissier. Above all else, players are expected to show military discipline, courage and fighting spirit. We want our footballers to go to war for us.

Alongside this patriotic vision of a dutiful and conformist team player, there is another Victorian trait that still influences English football — gentlemanly conduct. The globalisation of the Premier League has mixed a cocktail of playing styles into the English game, thus creating a fiery clash of cultures which in turn challenges and distorts our diluted Victorian sense of morality. At the very epicentre of this conflict is the old-fashioned and quintessentially English notion of "fair play". According to traditional English values, a player should never con a referee by diving on the floor or feigning injury.

However, our contemporary definition of "fair play" has evolved significantly. In the late nineteenth century, Victorian players would sometimes refuse to take a penalty, deeming it an unfair advantage to their team. During the mid-twentieth century, Leeds United and Juventus legend John Charles once stopped playing whilst he was clear through on goal because he wanted to check on the health of a player he'd just shoulder-barged to the floor.[4] These historic acts of noble chivalry may or may not have been representative of wider society at the time, but they would certainly be scoffed at today. When push comes to shove, gentlemanly conduct is no longer applicable to the modern era, as fans now expect players to manipulate referees and "be clever" in the box. Over time, our sensibilities evolve, as football's original Victorian mould is distorted and reshaped by the white-hot heat of repeated cultural shifts. Arguably, the increased financialisation and commercialisation of football has had the greatest impact upon fandom's psyche. A once strict and principled code of "fair play" has been slowly replaced by the pursuit of victory at any cost. In an increasingly complex world, our contemporary moral compass is spinning.

The Victorian footprint upon our footballing culture also

features some undesirable codes of conduct. A Victorian obsession with repressed sexual desire is still very much prevalent, as football is yet to shake off its longest running taboo — homosexuality. Tens of thousands of English professional footballers have played the game, yet only two have ever publicly come out as gay. In 1990, Justin Fashanu became the first. Consequently, he was vilified and struggled to get another playing contract in England. Eight years later, he tragically committed suicide. It's no wonder gay players live in silent fear. Wider society may have become increasingly tolerant, but football still remains chained to its repressive Victorian roots. Nevertheless, attempts are being made to loosen the grip. In the stands, homophobic chants have lessened over recent years (although they haven't disappeared fully) and clubs officially endorse LGBTQ+ groups. In May 2022, a watershed moment occurred when Blackpool player Jake Daniels bravely became the second English professional football player to publicly come out as gay. Whether or not he is an outlier for a new and progressive outlook on sexual freedom remains to be seen.

The nineteenth century is not done with us yet. The residue of Victorian notions of imperialism and white English superiority are still staining the psyche of English fandom. But these values have become increasingly undermined, as throughout the post-war period our Empire has been lost and England has become a multicultural country. Underneath the surface of civilised society, these changes stir a bubbling cauldron of resentment, humiliation and fear. All it takes is a small window of opportunity to present itself, and prejudices will soon reveal themselves. You can't kick racism out of football until you've kicked it out of society — it doesn't matter how many slogans you use. In the aftermath of England's Euro 2020 (or rather 2021) defeat, an onslaught of racist abuse was aimed at the young English "non-white" players who missed their penalty kicks. It was an incredibly depressing affair, and as much as fandom also condemned the attacks, the cauldron had bubbled over, revealing a divided and fractured *us*. The situation may have improved over recent decades — racist chanting has declined and is now frowned upon — but the problem hasn't gone away.

In August 2022, TV pundit Graham Souness was criticised for describing football as a "man's game".[5] In a later statement he corrected himself and rightly surmised that "football is a game for all".[6] Souness was not meaning to exclude women when he used that particular description, he was simply implying that football is a physical game and participants need to show strength, determination and bravery. It's a phrase he's been using his whole life, handed down by the Victorians, and no doubt it was said to him as a child. Nevertheless, the hot water in which Souness found himself is also evidence of our slow and progressive march away from the past. We are rapidly evolving, and within that process old ideas clash with new ones. Victorian society battled with the same dynamic.

The chains of the past are not easily loosened; English fandom is a rich tapestry of both progressive and regressive ideologies. The Victorians may have instilled within us virtues such as fair play, sporting integrity and gentlemanly conduct, but they also implanted remnants of white-British superiority, innate misogyny and sexual repression. Essentially, it's up to us to decide which traits we want to amplify the most.

Modern Fan Culture

As the beautiful game continues to evolve within the confines of an all-encompassing digital revolution, a number of different "types" of football supporters are developing alongside it. Previously, our footballing culture was dominated by traditional one-club supporters who followed their local team through thick and thin. Today, the picture is less clear because society is becoming increasingly complex, and therefore so are we. Football fan culture is now more diverse than ever, not just in gender, class or cultural aspects, but in the way people participate in the game. Attitudes and sensibilities are shifting, and perspectives are changing.

In July 2021, data research company Focaldata conducted a study on UK football supporters titled *Football Fandom in 2021*.[7] The report categorised modern fandom into five separate subtypes: Lifer, Statto, Expressionist, Socialiser and Game Changer. The research revealed that while traditional one-club supporters ("Lifers") were the most numerous, they constituted less than one-third of the surveyed population. As a technological revolution continues to play out, creating new forms of communication and consumer trends, people are finding new ways to connect with the beautiful game. Statto enthusiasts revel in analysing statistical data, while an Expressionist celebrates football's association with fashion, art and culture. Socialisers appreciate the community aspect of football, relishing its ability to bring people together and foster friendships. Game Changers find inspiration in the social impact of the game, particularly when footballers take moral stances on wider issues. Undoubtedly, football's appeal is expanding as individuals engage with the sport in increasingly diverse ways.

The research also revealed that one in five football supporters have absolutely no allegiance to any particular club. Will this trend accelerate? Perhaps so. With less than one-third of fans describing themselves as "Lifers", we seem to be evolving before our very eyes. There is no right or wrong way to connect with the beautiful game, but understanding why people relate to football is an important process for this book.

With just a passing interest, it's likely that casual supporters of the game will not be too interested in determining its governance. Therefore, for those who connect with football on a deeper, emotional level, the onus is on them to fight for systemic change. Only those who would class themselves as Lifers in this context are seriously affected by our governing bodies' lack of respect for fans. Although the economics of football continue to take the game further and further away from traditional supporters, they don't necessarily upset the wants of the Statto, Expressionist, Socialiser or Game Changer. This is an interesting dynamic — whilst football's popularity may be increasing, the deeper, more spiritual elements of it are being diluted. But do enough of us really care?

Like it or not, our fandom is evolving and the question of who we are is becoming is a pertinent one. With the formation of a European Super League looking increasingly likely in the long term, we must consider how many of us in England would actually want it to happen. Perhaps most of us reject the concept now in the mid-2020s, but that may change over time. Come 2030, who's to say that this would still be the case? If the ESL came into being, a Statto could still analyse data, Socialisers still have social events, Expressionists could still wear the latest clothing trends and Game Changers are unaffected. Undoubtedly, the impact of an ongoing technological revolution, the effects of commercialisation and the forces of globalisation are all combining to alter the footballing landscape. As powerful and globally revered monopolies continue to attract more and more support, our local football clubs suffer as a direct result, and this undermines the heritage of our traditional footballing pyramid. It bears a striking resemblance to the influx of multinational supermarkets which now dominate our high streets, resulting in longstanding local businesses being forced to close. Everywhere we turn, it seems that local is replaced by global. Could the consumer trend which sees shoppers increasingly put their money into multinational corporations be applied in a footballing context to the rise of "giant" (multinational) clubs?

When I began my teaching career in 2010, working in various primary schools throughout West Yorkshire, Leeds United were playing in the third tier. Within these schools, playgrounds were awash with the shirts of "elite" outfits such as Manchester United, Liverpool and Chelsea. There was hardly a Leeds top in sight, and it genuinely disappointed me. Despite this evidence being anecdotal, it's still relevant to the bigger picture. The young children of my city had turned their back upon their team, opting for a high-flying, glamourous Premier League club instead. Do we not see this pattern repeated over and over again throughout English towns and cities? For some supporters, a connection with an elite club may be a genuine local or family tie, but for others it has everything to do with them "being the best team" at the time of their initial engagement with football. Although the roots of such support could perhaps be labelled as "vacuous" or "superficial", it's still nevertheless a legitimate, and in truth quite substantial, component of the footballing landscape.

The lure of supporting a big club because they play the best football is not just a recent phenomenon. To extend this anecdotal evidence even further, I was recently watching a Liverpool match in a bar when I got chatting to a Liverpool fan with a Midlands accent. He was sitting with his 19-year-old son. I asked him why he supported Liverpool and not Wolverhampton Wanderers (his local team). He reasoned that when he was a child, in the 1970s, Liverpool were winning everything, and he always heard them on the radio. My heart sang when I learned his son was a season ticket holder at Wolves. The debate around why we support our respective clubs is not just pointless hair-splitting, it's vital in understanding our perspectives and our allegiances. Do we stick by our local clubs through thick and thin? Or do we just follow the highest level of football? Presently, it's arguably the former, but the shifting sands of time could alter that scenario.

For so many "traditional" fans, the whole point of following a football team is to feel a sense of belonging and a deep emotional connection. It's a ride consisting of highs and lows, backs to the wall and "us" against the world. Yes, we all want our teams to win, but what happens to that emotional connection when victory becomes too regular and too predictable? What happens to your psyche when your team is no longer the plucky underdog?

In recent years, supporters of oil-rich Manchester City have certainly become accustomed to winning football matches, with the club regularly amassing somewhere between 90 and 100 points a season. Surely you'd expect to see a bouncing stadium full of excited supporters for every home game, but this isn't always the case. In December 2021, an injury-depleted Leeds United made the short journey over the M62 to the Citizens' Eastlands home. Manchester City turned on the style and ran out comfortable 7–0 winners. However, what was most striking about the game (De Bruyne aside), was the mass exodus of home supporters prior to the final whistle. Videos from a perplexed away end captured the scenes of a half-empty stadium as the referee blew for full-time. Would this performance not typically induce fans to applaud their team off the pitch? Does a seven-goal masterclass not deserve to sustain attention levels until the end of the match?

Evidently, it seems the answer is no. After all, consumers expect results, and a goal-fest has now become a run-of-the-mill commodity to Manchester City home attendees. Victory is always satisfying, but it's not *that* exciting when it happens too regularly. How could it be? In our contemporary footballing landscape, it appears that for *some* supporters of constant winning machines, only defeat can be classed as truly emotional.

As football's regulation came to represent neoliberal principles, our perspectives have shifted alongside it. How many of us have come to embrace a Darwinian approach to football's competitive nature, as in big clubs are more worthy and smaller clubs should naturally be steamrollered? Football's early regulation insisted upon an egalitarian approach which protected smaller provincial towns from being dominated by larger urban centres. Should a tiny number of "super clubs" be allowed to permanently rise above the rest? Originally, English football was designed to never allow for such a dynamic.

The past and present tear us apart. Football was once managed in a way that promoted sporting integrity, equality and local community. Undoubtedly, the modern game is racing away from such principles. It feels like we are stuck somewhere in the middle. In order to understand our future direction of travel, one is compelled to think outside the parameters of individual club fanbases. The wider collective referred to as "English fandom" might be a lesser considered concept, but it's a vital one in the context of English football's bigger picture. Surely, the time has come to hold a mirror up to ourselves. Perhaps it's less a case of who we are and more a case of who we want to be?

Consciousness Inflation

Action is pointless; only senseless hope makes sense.
                    Mark Fisher, *Capitalist Realism*[1]

When comparing us to German fandom, with their established political movements, such as *Unsere Kurve* and 50+1 Stays!, it's difficult not to feel a little embarrassed by our obvious lack of action. Protesters sometimes stand outside their local stadiums holding banners and chanting, but it's always for a local cause, the wider system is never challenged. These passionate pockets of frustrated fans are segregated and disconnected from one another, focused upon their own club's battle and yet to develop a profound and present realisation: they're all fighting the same war.

Moreover, the media attention created by these isolated bouts of fan resistance only serves to highlight the profiteering individuals in question. From Malcom Glazer to Mike Ashley, media outlets portray these controversial individuals as pantomime villains, arrogantly dismissing a chorus of hisses and boos from a heavily partisan crowd. Very little coverage seems to point the finger at the private ownership model itself. Disgruntled fans are focused solely upon the removal of their respective owners rather than affording themselves space to propose plans for a viable successor, let alone challenge the overarching ownership framework. Indeed, an "anyone but them" mentality generates a sense of tunnel vision — supporters obviously want the "bad guys" out, but how do they even know that the successor will behave any differently? We may have developed organisations such as the Football Supporters Association (FSA), but they push for only minor reforms and don't have a membership base anywhere near capable of challenging the status quo.

Perhaps our lack of collective action has something to do with the deliberate destruction of class consciousness. In the 1970s, prior to the full marketisation of society, people were more aware of class divides. Today, class boundaries might be more fluid, but they are far from obsolete. However, the supposed eradication of class is beneficial to the ruling elite because it serves to atomise the individual, thus making it harder to engage in collective action. It's a process which has been decades in the making. As then Deputy Leader of the Labour Party John Prescott said in the lead up to the 1997 election, "We're all middle class now". Two years later, Tony Blair envisioned "a middle class that will include millions of people who traditionally may see themselves as working class, but whose ambitions are far broader than those of their parents and grandparents".[2] Ambition and aspiration have become the key terms used to convince us that society is now a level playing field in which those at the top achieved their status purely on merit. The overall message is clear: never resent the rich and powerful. Instead, turn your anger against those who aren't ambitious or hardworking enough because they're at fault, not the system.

In order to imagine new political possibilities, it's important to understand the structural causes of our social and economic constraints. The theorist Mark Fisher argued that neoliberalism is a scheme of "consciousness deflation"[3] — a project aimed at destroying competing schools of ideological thought "to the point of making them unthinkable".[4] It has been so successful in veiling itself as non-political that much of the general public now accept its draconian form of exploitative rule as the natural order of things. Fisher's theory of "reflexive impotence" also holds weight here.[5] It's a concept which suggests people feel they have no choice but to accept their fate, the feeling that one has gone too far down a certain road for change to be even possible — *it'll never happen anyway.* When you assess the situation in English football, does it not all feel like too much to overcome? This reflexive impotence excludes the possibility of political reform and ends up becoming a self-fulfilling prophecy. Our collective common sense wholeheartedly believes that nothing can be done to change football for the better, therefore nothing will be done and the downward spiral of deflated expectations, resentment and inaction reinforces itself.

Many of us bemoan the "state of the game", but this deeply rooted cynicism is counterproductive because it fortifies a wider sense of pessimism. This notion is championed by political activist Mariame Kaba, as she argues that cynicism often prevents people from believing in genuine transformative change:

> When dealing with oppressive systems, cynicism is a begrudging allegiance, extracted from people whose minds could otherwise open new doors, make new demands, and conjure visions of what a better world could look like.[6]

Does our cynicism camouflage a moral and intellectual retreat? The fact that there have been no major uprisings against the system is evidence of our "begrudging allegiance" with it. A counter-revolution would need to set its sights on our collective imagination and allow us to realise that economic change in football is actually possible. As Keir Milburn explains, a process of "consciousness inflation" includes the increased confidence and capacity that comes with seeing yourself as part of a powerful collective actor rather than an isolated individual. And it also includes that expansion of social and political possibility that comes when what is presented as necessary and inevitable is revealed as merely contingent and therefore, in principle, changeable.[7]

In this reality, senseless hope becomes pointless and action becomes necessary. The question of how to form that powerful collective actor will come later, but first we'll consider an example of how this pervasive pessimism limits our imagination and what we define as possible.

The Crouch Report

Football's current economic trajectory spells doom for *so* many clubs that even the most ardent supporters of free-market fundamentalism understand the need for reform. The very fact that a Tory government deemed it necessary to politically intervene in the governance of football is testimony to just how bad the current economic climate really is, but it's also evidence of a shift in the Overton Window.

In 2021, the government commissioned a report by Tracey Crouch MP titled *Fan-Led Review of Football Governance: Securing the Game's Future*.[8] Referred to as *The Crouch Report*, it provided an opportunity for the Tory party to ride a wave of populist backlash against the European Super League (the demise of both Bury and Macclesfield was not deemed important enough to trigger a review). *The Crouch Report* listed 47 recommendations, including an independent regulator; a "shadow board" so fans can have some say over off-field matters; and a more even distribution of wealth lower down the pyramid. Although these recommendations are well-meaning, they're also evidence of English fandom appealing for concessions from a higher power that it dares not properly challenge. Even if the recommendations were to be considered in Parliament, they'd be severely watered down by MPs that are lobbied by the powers that be. The report is a diversion in the sense that it doesn't pay enough attention to the systemic causation of fandom's suffering. In fact, every single recommendation reveals a "begrudging allegiance", in Kaba's term, with the overarching economic system. Rather ironically, various journalists and people involved in football described *The Crouch Report* as a "once in a lifetime opportunity" to change football.[9]

The fact that fan-led reviews like *The Crouch Report*, or fan groups such as the FSA, are not operating external to the current system's ideological parameters is concerning. Without structural change, the same problems will still exist. *The Crouch Report* is representative of a wider inability to question the validity of privatisation and free-market economics within the sporting realm. Such a report is better defined by the questions it doesn't ask and the debates it doesn't trigger. As Maurizio Lazzarato suggests, "Those who govern have the power to define problems and formulate questions which they define as 'the possibilities'".[10] By commissioning *The Crouch Report*, the neoliberals are controlling the limits of revolt and further consolidating their power. There are other ways to govern football, in fact we previously had regulation in place that protected the interests of supporters. Therefore, the report *should* begin with a particular question, and one that may shed some light upon English football's current predicament: What happened to Rule 34? The premise of Rule 34 should be central to any commissioned report that intends to address English football's flippant disregard for supporters. It's important to be aware of a constant process of faux reinvention — indeed, this is partly why neoliberalism has survived for so long. It offers the illusion of change, however in reality the economic principles that underpin it are always maintained. Indeed, the political will for reform may have arrived, but it's wholly defined by neoliberal modes of thinking. Unfortunately, the good intentions of the fans who contributed to *The Crouch Report* have been made to unwittingly serve the interests of the status quo.

Sleepwalking Towards the Future

Now let's turn directly to the question of football's current trajectory — the ongoing process of monopolisation and the looming shadow of a European Super League.

The passionate demonstrations in the wake of the initial ESL announcement do at least provide some optimism that a well-organised movement can potentially prevail. These protests offer proof that the wider footballing community currently harbours passionate resistance to the formation of a closed-shop elite league. Furthermore, through their protestations, fans showed they were willing to overlook club rivalries in the fight for justice. This is powerful stuff. Nevertheless, whilst the reaction of fans triggered a major U-turn, with the ESL project being swiftly abandoned by English clubs, behind the scenes preparations are being made for another attempt at launching an ESL, and previous mistakes will be learned from. Over time, if the monopolisation process is allowed to continue, the odds are stacked in favour of a European Super League emerging.

It's important to remember what the economic system is veering towards. In December 2023, the European Court of Justice ruled that UEFA and FIFA both acted "unlawfully" by blocking the breakaway tournament when it initially launched. In a reaction to this landmark ruling, the company backing the European Super League agenda, A22, ironically declared that "football is free".[11] Could their shambolic first attempt at an ESL even be a clever psychological ploy? The very concept of a European Super League has now been thrust into the conscious (and legal) realm of possibility, and therefore from here on in its advocates will attempt to normalise the concept over time. We've certainly all become more familiar with the idea of a European Super League since its announcement. Could this not be deemed a successful first step in a longer process?

We must ask ourselves what we as fans can actually do in the long term to stop the ESL from being implemented. What can we realistically achieve within the parameters of the current system? Worryingly, the answer is very little. Half of England's "big six" clubs involved with the initial ESL project are owned by US businessmen who will be chomping at the bit to get the proposal over the line, despite what they may claim to the contrary. English fandom has no say in the governance of English football, therefore should we not be looking to build a new system of governance that grants us a measure of control?

A movement to prevent English clubs from joining the ESL cannot simply rely on passion. It needs to be coordinated, calculated and targeted. A hastily organised protest was enough to stave off the first attempt, but in the long run it won't be sufficient. If we're caught off guard by a second and better prepared ESL attempt, unplanned protests are likely to fall apart very quickly or be tarnished by acts of desperation and violence on behalf of the protestors, allowing them to be branded as "extremist" by clickbait media outlets. Contrary to the aims of those protesting, this in turn would serve to normalise the ESL yet further and present the concept as a mainstream and palatable solution to the advancement of football in Europe.

There can be no doubt that the ESL would be an attractive proposition to many football followers across the globe. The biggest clubs in Europe playing one another on a regular basis is inarguably an exciting prospect. True, when you're watching an overseas league, the "big teams" add a greater sense of importance and feel more worthy of your time. For this reason, we should expect, without malice, the billions of people who watch the global giants of our game to be receptive to welcoming a European Super League, as they have no particular allegiance to our localities, traditions or cultural heritage. However, we do, at least for now.

Perspectives shift over time and are influenced greatly by wider events. Moving forward, an increasing number of English football fans may be attracted to the ESL model as the competitive nature of our top flight diminishes. Nevertheless, the first attempt to form a European Super League is a good example of an event that happened to bring English fandom closer together. A unanimous response from millions of football fans unearthed our commonality and our shared experience. It created a bond of solidarity, if only a short-lived one. Could we unite again? The question about whether English fandom has the capacity to develop into a united political movement is an important one. At the very least, such a question aims to trigger a process of "consciousness inflation" thus extending the parameters of our collective imagination and opening the door to new possibilities.

Building a Political Movement

Every revolutionary idea — in science, politics, art or whatever
— seems to evoke three stages of reaction. They may be summed
up by the phrases:
   (1) It's completely impossible, don't waste my time.
   (2) It's possible, but not worth doing.
   (3) I said it was a good idea all along.

Arthur C. Clarke, The Promise of Space

Football unites as much as it divides. Our clubs bridge communities and bring people together in a shared experience. The cultural and social bonds created through football transcend traditional barriers of class, race, gender and religion. Why couldn't these bonds be used for the purposes of political affiliation? Today, there exists a growing frustration amongst a large population of politically homeless football supporters. The governance of our national game has overlooked millions of passionate fans, and so too has the governance of our national economy. Imagine if an idea took hold, one that even transcended longstanding club rivalries. A very big idea, focused on uniting hundreds of passionate fanbases against an oppressive system. As the saying goes, your enemy's enemy is your friend. The wider cultural phenomenon that this book has defined as "English fandom" is a very interconnected network involving millions of people who communicate regularly. Within this readymade network, an appealing political idea could spread fast. Seeds grow, and our footballing culture is the ideal petri dish.

The first step towards growing this metaphorical seed would be to initiate a proof of concept. This would take the form of some non-league clubs adopting the status of a Public-Common Partnership in alliance with their local authority. If a small number of clubs in the lower tiers of the pyramid proved that the PCP concept works in football, then proposals could be drawn up for when a league club goes bankrupt. If the initial trials of footballing PCPs were successful, then this could convince fans that the idea would work on a wider scale. Consequently, an organisation which sought to implement PCPs at the national level would grow in numbers.

But what would need to happen in order to force the agenda politically? At the time of writing, polls predict an incoming Labour government at the next general election. One possible approach would be to create supporters' movements demanding that the government takes a role in fostering PCPs for football in the way outlined above. This would depend on the government wanting to break with neoliberal models and upset wealthy elites — something few governments, even those on the left, have shown themselves as keen to do. But suppose in an ideal world we had a crusading and transformative Labour Party in power that was fully signed up to the agenda. What should the manifesto be?

A targeted state-investment plan would be used to overhaul the entire English football industry. It would be possible to incorporate the following goals into one single Act of Parliament. However, in order to ensure the transition into public ownership is as smooth as possible, it would be more practical to create separate Acts of Parliament for each independent aim. This approach would allow each Act to be legally watertight, thus meaning that future counterattacks from the legal teams of dispossessed owners would be harder to create. It would also ensure that legal challenges only applied to specific Acts and didn't derail the wider process of nationalisation. According to the thesis of this book, our state-investment plan would include:

- All English football clubs being purchased and transformed into Public-Common Partnerships.
- The creation of a wider Public-Common Partnership acting as an umbrella company for selected manufacturing processes and other PCPs.
- The complete takeover of all governing bodies related to English football.
- Transference of all commercial rights relating to broadcasting (these could be easily reassigned at the end of a contract cycle).
- A ban on sponsorship (this may be subject to compensation claims from existing contractors).
- Transference of all commercial rights for shirt production (this may be subject to compensation claims from existing contractors).
- A newly designed digital tech platform capable of delivering live English football to every country in the world.
- The formation of a public social media company.
- The creation of a public gambling company (or companies).
- A network of public breweries capable of developing and delivering products to domestic and international markets.
- A network of factories for replica shirt manufacturing.
- A stimulus package to cover costs until this new collectively owned sector becomes profitable.

Because the combined cost of football clubs is up for parliamentary debate, the negotiations would begin immediately. The aim is that a financial settlement with private owners would be reached as soon as possible, although a deadline would need to be imposed. To help pay for the lawful acquisition of our clubs, an online public gambling company would be created with immediate effect. In addition to this, the public brewery would be established in order to begin its commercial operations as soon as possible. Furthermore, the development of a highly sophisticated digital tech platform must also begin straight away. Because broadcasting rights would provide the main source of income, the establishment of a worldwide digital broadcasting service is vital in making this fledgling footballing sector profitable. Once fully operational, the profits generated from this service alone could easily fund football as a public service. In fact, the annual profits garnered through 200 million people paying into a monthly subscription programme would approximately match the combined cost of all our football clubs. Initially, the state would be making a sizable financial outlay to purchase our clubs and cover costs for the first couple of seasons. However, such is the worldwide popularity of English football that the initial state investment could be paid back (with interest) in a relatively short timeframe.

Playing the Game of Politics

Supposing, as seems likely, we can't get an incoming government to react sympathetically to our plans. The question would then be whether serious political pressure can be sustained via the formation of a political party.

Recent political history has proven that outright democratic victory is not always needed to successfully push through a political agenda. Despite a lack of elected MPs, UKIP still managed to create enough political pressure to achieve Brexit. The Leave campaign utilised the (controversial) public relations techniques of Edward Bernays, which involved a US-style polarisation along identity lines. It was a cleverly conducted and emotionally charged project of anti-establishment populism. Alternatively, the Remain camp naively made the mistake of merely highlighting "rational" arguments. Just like the election of US President Donald Trump, Britain's exit from the EU sent a huge shockwave across the political landscape. Interestingly, despite our economic foundations being left-leaning, this hypothetical revolution does draw intriguing parallels with the successful Brexit campaign. Both agendas share ideological common ground: self-determination, national sovereignty and a desire to be free of unelected foreign rule.

So what would our political party look like? It could be a single-issue party focused exclusively on "Taking Back Football". In the context of a Labour government already moving toward new forms of public ownership, trying to force their hand with regards to putting football on the agenda could be successful. If we could challenge Labour in Red Wall constituencies (which are less politically consistent than they were previously) then political pressure would grow. The possibility of protest votes from football fans across marginals could force Labour to incorporate nationalising football to neutralise the threat to their narrow majorities.

In the absence of any future governments on either left or right taking a new approach to public ownership, a political party focused on pushing the public ownership agenda for key utilities could be another way to drag reluctant politicians into more radical territory. Public ownership is extremely popular with the electorate across all so-called political divides. A poll conducted by *Survation* for We Own It in 2022 showed that a majority of the UK public support public ownership of key utilities. For example, 62% of Conservative voters want to see energy in public ownership, whilst 68% of Conservative voters want water to be nationalised.[1] Public ownership is popular across all income levels, ages, genders and in all regions of the UK (rather like football itself). This means that a political party focused on bringing key utilities plus football —which I hope this book has demonstrated is more like a public good than a commodity — into public ownership could take votes from *both* major parties everywhere in the UK.

In order to succeed, this idea needs to appeal to voters from across the political spectrum. Moreover, it would be beneficial to have the major political parties onside as opposed to adversaries. Due to its broad and extremely ambitious agenda, it's likely that from the outset it could only be adopted in full by an entirely new party, however campaigns normalise demands over time and create pressure through popular support. If it developed a broad enough appeal, the establishment of a new party could be the means to eventually get these proposals adopted in full by mainstream political parties. Without a shift to proportional representation, the likelihood of achieving outright electoral victory is incredibly slim. But this doesn't necessarily mean that an independent party can't achieve its goals over time.

There is one particular electoral circumstance that would suit our agenda perfectly. If a general election was to produce a hung parliament, it's possible that a small number of MPs could exert extraordinary power. In such a case, public ownership of football becomes a political reality if the party achieves a certain number of elected MPs. The Democratic Unionist

Party (DUP) have illustrated how much power only ten elected MPs can wield in a political landscape that harbours no clear majority. If it meant seizing power, a coalition could potentially allocate the tiny percentage of GDP necessary to take football into public ownership. Our economic rationale must be clear, concise and fully costed. An "oven-ready" deal, so to speak.

But how could this political message begin to establish itself? We are living in an age of "post-truth" in which people are sceptical of statistics. A deep sense of exhaustion and mistrust exists throughout our political landscape when people are exposed to data, particularly so if it contradicts our favoured agenda. Today, it's powerful and emotional stories that dominate proceedings, not the assurance of raw evidence. We appear to be living through a period of "de-enlightenment", whereby scientific methodology is increasingly sidelined. Any emerging political movement should account for such a transition and not become too focused on statistics. A successful campaign should understand that data is useful, but only when it underpins an emotive narrative.

Left-wingers may be more inclined to agree with the principles of this argument and are more inspired by the idea of building a revolutionary movement which defies neoliberal economic policy. As Keir Milburn suggests, those on the left are better suited to "active" events. As he explains, "These are events which their participants experience as something that they have constructed with others. This tends to cause an expansion of social and political possibility."[2] By contrast, due to the movement's left-leaning economic rationale, those on the right will be harder to win over. Therefore it's important to recognise and understand what motivates those belonging to this political school of thought. Corey Robin defines conservatism as "a meditation on — and theoretical rendition of — the felt experience of having power, seeing it threatened, and trying to win it back".[3] Therefore in order to successfully appeal to typical right-wing voters, the movement to nationalise football must trigger a sense of loss within the psyche of English fandom in connection with the state of the modern game. Similar to the aforementioned (and successful) Brexit campaign, the movement would need a slogan that generates an emotional response. Dominic Cummings' "Take Back Control" — which spearheaded the Leave campaign's marketing message — proved to be a very shrewd psychological ploy. Initially, it was "Take Control", but the addition of "back" helped induce a nostalgia that convinced people Britain's former position was superior. Cleverly, it generated a sense of loss. However, a movement should also be wary of unleashing the potentially dangerous concept of nostalgic nationalism.

In 2006, Nigel Farage was a political outsider, yet come 2016 he had successfully fronted a populist movement which catapulted his vision right into the centre ground of UK politics. What Farage had of course was wealthy backers, a media background that had been stoking fear of immigration for years, a set of MPs receptive to his agenda and good access to mainstream media (despite the continual underperformance of his party). Alternatively, a political agenda which sought to drastically undermine a network of influential billionaires would be operating in the face of a very likely hostile media and establishment. But this movement doesn't need to create division. It's about forming unity through our footballing culture, and an emancipatory framework is in fact available: public ownership is a superior model — this should always be a main focus.

This book cannot afford to dwell upon whether or not Brexit has been a success or failure, and nor shall it. Suffice to say that the very word "Brexit" can often trigger an emotional response from people on both sides of the argument. Nevertheless, Brexit can only be viewed as a positive step forward in the prospective nationalisation of English football. This is because from inside the European Union, such a transition would be deemed illegal due to the EU's liberalisation laws.

Article 3 of The Treaty on the Functioning of the European Union (TFEU) declares that the "Union shall have exclusive competence in the establishing of the competition rules necessary for the functioning of the internal market".[4] In basic English, this means that establishing any state-owned monopoly could be deemed illegal because it is anti-competitive and does not adhere to market principles. In fact, Article 106(3) specifically entrusts the commission with a surveillance duty "in the case of public undertakings and undertakings which states grant special or exclusive rights".[5] Therefore, if the UK was still a member of the EU, then any plan to take football clubs and broadcasting, etc. into the public realm could face a number of legal roadblocks. Consequently, club owners and broadcasting moguls would appeal to the European Courts, thus making the whole process a messy, drawn-out affair. In this context, Brexit has stripped away a lot of red tape and complex bureaucracy, therefore making English football's potential transition from private to public a lot smoother.

However, there is FIFA regulation which specifically prevents government interference into football associations. Although, as is usually the case with FIFA, it doesn't exactly stand up to scrutiny. Article 15(c) of the FIFA Statutes states: "national association statutes are to be independent and avoid any form of political interference".[6] This makes little sense because FIFA's system of governance is itself a

form of political interference. In truth, the ruling essentially protects the corrupt practices of leading officials. FIFA has faced accusations of bribery and fraud, especially following the public prosecutions of 2015, which exposed pervasive corruption within the organisation. Leading figures have seemingly strengthened their grip on power by exchanging cash for votes. It's a system mired in controversy and financial corruption. The irony is that FIFA's associated members are required to comply with "principles of good governance".

FIFA has promptly threatened countries with expulsion whenever their governments have initiated investigations into FIFA's shadowy practices. As a result, this non-intervention principle has become closely associated with shielding a network of corruption that FIFA itself has cultivated. Moreover, this ruling is rather inconsistently applied. Mali, Kenya and Pakistan have all faced banning orders recently for "third party interference". However, when France and Italy's respective governments decided to abandon FIFA's regulations regarding player agents and impose their own guidelines under federal law, FIFA took absolutely no action. Surely such measures could only be deemed as "third party interference"? There is also the obvious fact that China's Football Federation is fully controlled by central government. So if FIFA insists that football associations must be free from political influence, then why is China afforded such privilege?

The reality is that FIFA enforces this regulation whenever it best suits them. China has expressed an interest in hosting a World Cup before 2050 and FIFA is keen on tapping into that prospective market. In an unstable financial system, the expense of hosting such a tournament means that only a handful of countries are putting themselves forward. Could an English bid to host a future World Cup shield us from this

politically motivated legislation? Perhaps so. Either way, FIFA's shambolic governance of international football provides an opportunity to build political pressure and strike at the very heart of the establishment. Their misdemeanours have made them into a global laughing stock and a serious challenge to their authority is long overdue. If FIFA were to rule that the nationalisation of English football breached regulations, then they would need to answer the Chinese question, which of course they wouldn't be able to do.

Making a Trust Leap

Public ownership of football is a new concept, and as a result many people would initially be wary of it. Collectively, we would need to make what Rachel Botsman describes as a "trust leap". The fear of the unknown is not easily overcome. Nevertheless, the credibility of governing authorities is waning, and with a general loss of confidence in football's wider financial system, these circumstances create room for the emergence of new ideas. It would be difficult to argue that our contemporary footballing landscape isn't fertile ground for revolution. If a bolder and better economic plan can be wrapped up in a well-positioned narrative, then surely the fear of economic transition can be lessened. Trust in new forms of governance is often propelled by advancements in technology or the decline of outdated ideologies. As Botsman explains:

> Trust leaps expand what is possible, what we can invent and who can be inventor. Trust leaps extend the reach of our collaboration and creations, opening up new horizons of opportunity. That is why trust matters so much and why establishing confidence in the unknown has been a central

part of innovation and economic development over the course of history.[7]

In order for the public to make a trust leap, then certain hurdles need to be overcome. Botsman believes that a successful trust leap can be summarised in three steps:

1) Making the unfamiliar more familiar.
2) Locating the "what's in it for me" (WIIFM) factor.
3) Acquiring effective trust influencers.[8]

So can the potential public ownership of football be applied to this model? The first step can be aided with a touch of virtuous (and admittedly populist) nostalgia. Historically speaking, community ownership and Rule 34 are familiar; over a century of community-run football serves to confirm this. Our football clubs are already romanticised in our cultural consciousness and essentially (and rather ironically) the unfamiliar is actually the foreign-based dictatorships controlling our clubs. This is one angle that should be tentatively pursued. Through this filter, we see that we are in fact the moderate viewpoint, with the system itself taking on the role of an unjust and extreme movement. Additionally, the more public ownership is discussed, the more familiar it becomes in the public consciousness. Wrapping the narrative in a blanket of historic footballing nostalgia would certainly aid the revolution's cause.

Secondly, the WIIFM factor is obvious. Ownership rights, democratic procedure, employment opportunities, affordable matchday tickets, upgraded infrastructure and closer community bonds are all tangible benefits of embracing this proposed system of governance. Public ownership is empowering, and *all* football fans have lots to gain if it can be realised. In this way, a new and exciting model would, by default, have a WIIFM factor at the forefront of its manifesto.

Thirdly, the world of football is very interconnected and harbours great potential for celebratory influencers to help galvanise a passionate political movement. Ex-players, TV pundits, presenters, podcasters, actors, comedians, musicians and journalists could harness their deep connection to the game and invite the masses to stand against the political and commercial tyranny currently pervading football — their opinions could impact millions of politically homeless and frustrated fans. Today, we tend to prioritise the viewpoints of our online echo chambers over government spokespeople or "so-called experts". Such is the power of celebrity that a small number simply discussing the potentiality of public ownership could swell the movement's numbers.

The power of celebrity could also be utilised in another way. Because of football's overwhelming popularity throughout the arts, there may be ample opportunities to raise millions of pounds through the UK's cultural sector. What if a small collection of high-profile musicians agreed to perform at a charity gig in aid of the movement? Organising just one medium-sized music festival would provide the party with huge levels of funding. Having worked in the comedy industry for over a decade, I know a lot of football-obsessed comedians who could shift a few tickets at a one-off event. Perhaps a political movement centred around freeing our national sport from commercial profiteers has huge strategic advantages in raising funds.

Finally, the formation of a European Super League represents the perfect mechanism for generating a sense of loss. Essentially, this would destroy English football as we know it. Moreover, the economics are telling — the ESL will happen — it is simply a matter of when. If others can be convinced of this inescapable truth, then more may flock to the banner of counter-revolution before it is too late. As the ESL formally materialises, people will look for ideas that challenge its implementation, therefore we need to offer a coherent solution prior to the event. In fact, the anger and fear generated in the wake of a second official ESL attempt may be capable of clearing the psychological fog and readying the collective for political action. Therefore it's important to act ahead of the curve and have a viable notion of future governance already immersed into the public consciousness. It's probable that the development of a second formal ESL attempt will happen incrementally (English clubs would be compelled to join eventually), allowing the transition to feel more naturalised and inevitable as the monopolisation process distorts people's mindsets. However, in the grand scheme of things, the scheduling of the ESL's inauguration matters not. We have been humiliated for too long — it's time to counterattack.

Conclusion
Withdraw Your Consent

It's easier to fool people than to convince them that they have been fooled.

Mark Twain

The politics of wider society and the politics of football are not mutually exclusive. The unyielding march of financialisation has undermined democracy, transferring power away from ordinary people and over to a cartel of financial elites who control the media, influence politicians and dictate the wider economic agenda. In what appears to be a permanent fiscal crisis, severe austerity measures are inflicted upon entire populations as economic policy is subordinated to service huge, financially crippling debt repayments. Like helpless hatchlings in a nest, nation states beg for the attention of an unrestricted pool of private capital by sacrificing and commodifying their national sovereignty: health, education, transport, natural resources and just about everything you can think of has been or is being privatised. Multinational corporations grow increasingly powerful, caring not for wider society or planetary boundaries. We're all locked inside this cycle, unable to break free.

We can see this process impacting English football. From giant US investment firms to petro-dollar states in the Middle

East, England's biggest clubs have been brought to market and sold to foreign financial elites. This all-powerful pool of private capital now plays a defining role in our national game, as football's governing bodies stand idly by. And so do *we*.

Footballing culture in this country may be unique, but its distinctiveness is coming under sustained attack. The all-encompassing force of globalised commercialism is destroying our unique heritage and replacing it with a vacuous void: a soulless market of empty consumerism. Our own identity — which has been appropriated, repackaged and sold back to us — is becoming an ever-grainier image. Ultimately, we too are being warped by the immense gravity of this commercialised void as it alters our attitudes and mindsets. Consumers, trapped inside a prison of no alternatives.

This book has attempted to unlock the door. Only from outside the prison walls can you make sense of the bigger picture. Subliminally controlled by the "invisible hand" of market fundamentalism, *we* accept a reality in which the pursuit of profit is paramount and competition trumps cooperation. It's a debunked economic theory that erroneously assumes self-interest as the predominant force in human nature. According to its doctrine, notions such as loyalty, community, pride, self-respect, honour, love and commitment to a wider cause, are all presumed to be playing second fiddle. However, these forces are often the biggest drivers in our behaviour, particularly in a footballing context. You don't travel hundreds of miles on a Tuesday night to watch your team play against superior opposition because it is in your "self-interest" to do so. Obviously, there are other motivating factors at play. Considering the circumstances outlined in Part 1, self-respect is perhaps the most important, because nobody can save *us* except *ourselves*.

Unite and Rule

In November 2021, whilst playing in the fifth tier, Notts County had over 12,000 fans pile through the turnstiles.[1] Many top division clubs across Europe don't receive that amount of support. Only in England is this possible — a non-league side with those spectator numbers is what makes us unique. Every country has big teams, but we have something else entirely — hundreds of lower league clubs, each with a deeply passionate support base and each as important as the next.

We Brits are very good at creating and exporting culture. Whether it's sport, music, comedy or screen, our creations are celebrated across the entire globe. That's why protecting our historic footballing heritage is so important. A big part of the reason why English football is so popular worldwide is due to a network of passionate fan bases, all of which combine to make-up *the* original footballing culture — it can't be replicated anywhere else. In so many respects, we are the unique selling point of English football. Therefore it's vital that stadiums are filled with those who live and die for their clubs. Ironically, we'll need to de-commercialise English football in order to create a better commercial product for overseas subscribers to enjoy.

We have forgotten our own importance. When a child is filmed clambering up stadium steps for the first time, you see that they're totally gobsmacked, and it makes our hearts sing to see that magic written across their face. But we need to be aware of something significant: it's not the actual football or even the players who make that impression. The child is in awe of the people and the scale of our togetherness: the fans, the collective, the noise and the atmosphere. It is us, the *people* of the people's game that instil that wonder.

In their book *The Dawn of Everything*, David Graeber and David Wengrow discuss "schismogenesis", a term coined in the 1930s by the archaeologist Gregory Bateson "to describe people's tendency to define themselves against one another".[2] Instead of defining themselves by what they have in common with each other, in schismogenesis individuals or groups define themselves *in opposition to others*, deliberately behaving differently from neighbouring counterparts and accentuating their differences to purposefully create separation.[3] But when we consider English fandom, we see the exact reverse of this tendency. In fact, far from exaggerating differences, fanbases imitate and mimic one another constantly. We all sing exactly the same songs and behave in exactly the same manner. We constantly celebrate each other but do so with a very British sense of humour, mocking and goading one another like squabbling siblings competing for attention. Open your eyes, we're all cut from the same cloth. Our tribal allegiances and our fierce rivalries are merely surface level, underneath it all there exists a deep bond between us, a commonality that must be brought out into the open and celebrated. Through all the bravado, the gesturing and the piss-taking, we need each other — we are each other. We've all met a friend of a friend who declared in conversation that they're not interested in football, and I bet your heart sank. It doesn't really matter who you support, it only matters how you support. Passion, loyalty and commitment, the very best qualities of human nature — we share them.

A lion yet to awaken, English fandom is a force more powerful than it knows. Through football we could drive deep societal change by creating an ethical economic system which promotes togetherness, a philosophy in which spirituality and localness overcome commercialism and globalisation. There would be tangible economic, political and social benefits, too. The idea of redirecting football's huge revenue streams back towards the public realm is an exciting prospect. We could be granted a larger share of our national economy and a huge dollop of political clout through the collective ownership of several influential corporations. Not to mention the shared ownership of our beloved football clubs. Moving forward, the investment of patient capital and long-term strategic planning in our national economy must replace the cost-cutting, job-slashing and general short-termism of Thatcherite financialisation. Creating a collectively owned manufacturing sector through the football industry would provide a sturdy stepping stone for such a transition.

It's time to put the white flag down and mobilise. A national sport belongs to a nation. "It's just a game", people tell you, unaware of how deeply it makes us feel. But maybe that's the whole point of this book, it *is* "just a game", so why can't the political structure be easily reorganised? Nobody needs to be flown on a plane to Rwanda or have their human rights violated, we just need to make a small selection of rich and powerful people a little less rich and powerful. Isn't achieving such a goal already part of most people's political playbook?

Clearly, this game we love is more than "just a game" to us. In fact, for millions of people all around the globe, football represents a faith, and just like any other faith, it requires belief. In our everyday conversations we talk about winning the next match, keeping the good run going or turning the bad run around. Maybe next season will be our year? It's the lowest-scoring sport in the world and that's what makes it so special, because when you boil it all down to its purest form, football is about hope. It's about believing that you *can* win, no matter who you're up against.

The true extent of the people's shame is best measured by our lack of fight; our political passivity; our begrudging allegiance with the system. English fandom must not be defined by helplessness, so I'll leave the ball in your court. This book is not claiming to have all the answers to our problems, it is simply suggesting that we step away from hopelessness, and in doing so forge a new path towards the future. A path which leads *us* back to the people's game.

Acknowledgements

The writing of this book began as a solo project but quickly turned into a huge collaborative effort. The first person I'd like to thank is Ryan Murray. Luckily, I hired you as an editor and for 12 months we worked on this project together. For every sentence I emailed over, you wrote a paragraph and your tutoring helped mould me into a far better writer. Furthermore, your deep and extensive footballing knowledge proved to be hugely beneficial in the early stages of this book.

A massive thank you must be extended to Keir Milburn. After finding out about your work with PCPs, I went about contacting you for assistance with creating a public ownership model for English football. As luck would have it, you're a fellow Leeds United fan, which probably explains why you afforded me a couple of hours in a city centre bar as I ranted incessantly about this idea. As far as political deliberations go, I don't belong anywhere near a man of your intellect and stature so I'm incredibly grateful that you gave me that Sunday afternoon. Perhaps the biggest turning point for this project was securing a publishing deal with Repeater Books — a publishing deal that you made happen. I am forever in your debt.

I'd like to say a huge thank you to my second editor, Carl Neville. The impact you've made on this book cannot be overstated. Your knowledge, expertise and patience are very much appreciated. From the off, you knew more about what I was trying to achieve than I did and if this book has any claim to a measured tone, then it is only because of you. With your vast experience, you've reformatted the entire book and still managed to make me feel like I was controlling things. After a few personal errors of judgement, I came to realise that it was far better for the project if I just accepted whatever you suggested as gospel. Being a part of your working schedule has been a huge privilege.

A huge amount of appreciation must also be extended towards Josh Turner and Christopher DeVeau. Your expert copyediting skills have made this text worthy of publication, and your superb editorial advice has improved the book significantly.

I'm also very grateful to a couple of highly acclaimed football journalists who gladly gave their time and expertise to a stranger on the internet. Over a two-year period, Kieran Maguire and Nick Harris provided regular email correspondence without expecting anything in return, their contribution has been invaluable. Thank you to Jamie Borthwick for a great piece on Hearts FC and to Phil Hay who made the connection. Thanks to Chris Taylor (LUFCDATA) for providing me with a range of statistics, Ian King for his contribution and Patricio Miller for an excellent piece regarding Argentinian footballing culture. Thanks to Kai Heron and Sam Perry for sending me relevant articles. A big thanks to Matt Zarb-Cousin for your expert political advice across a range of subject matters. Thank you to everyone at Repeater Books who played a contributory role in the writing and production of this book and thanks to all those friends (and family) who've read draft chapters or allowed me to bounce ideas off them.

I must extend my gratitude towards Marcelo Bielsa, the greatest teacher I have ever known — your lessons will last a lifetime.

Finally, the biggest thank you of all goes to my long-suffering partner, Rachel. When nobody listened to my online presentations about changing football, it was you that suggested I should write a book. At the time, neither of us could have known how much "that book" would take from our family life, and how much you would have to pick up the slack. I'm forever grateful for your love and support. To my two beautiful children, Isobel and Joel, I'm so sorry that daddy couldn't play, but I was writing this. I hope one day you'll read it and feel proud.

Endnotes

PART 1
The People's Game

1   Mickaël Correia (2023) *A People's History of Football* (London: Pluto Books), p. 5.
2   Quoted in Oliver Kay, "If Barcelona can't sign Messi and PSG can, what does that tell us after ten years of FFP?", *The Athletic*, 12 August 2021.
3   Correia, *A People's History of Football*, p. 34.
4   Rachel Botsman (2017) *Who Can You Trust?: How Technology Brought Us Together and Why It Might Drive Us Apart* (New York: PublicAffairs), p. 40.
5   Quoted in Phil Hay (2022) *And It Was Beautiful: Marcelo Bielsa and the Rebirth of Leeds United* (London: Seven Dials), p. 17.

The Neoliberal Takeover

1   David Conn, "Follow the Money", *London Review of Books*, Vol. 34: No. 16, 30 August 2012, https://www.lrb.co.uk/the-paper/v34/n16/david-conn/follow-the-money
2   Quoted in Adrian Tempany, *And the Sun Shines Now: How Hillsborough and the Premier League Changed Britain* (London: Faber), p. 145.
3   Ibid., p. 50.
4   Ibid., p. 54.
5   Ibid., p. 254.

Rise of the Monopolies

1 James Plunkett, *End State: 9 Ways Society is Broken – and how we can fix it* (London: Hachette), p. 26.

2 Quoted in Justin Sherman, "The Devil's Odyssey: How Silvio Berlusconi Turned AC Milan into a Superpower", *These Football Times*, 19 August 2019.

3 Declan Harte, "How much does AFC Bournemouth's squad cost compare to all other Championship sides?", *Football League World*, 21 April 2022, https://footballleagueworld.co.uk/how-much-does-afc-bournemouths-squad-cost-compare-to-all-other-championship-sides

4 "Net debt of clubs in the Premier League and EFL Championship from 2017 to 2022", *Statista*, June 2023, https://www.statista.com/statistics/1336333/net-debt-premier-league-championship-clubs

5 Oliver Young-Myles, "Championship clubs spending 'unsustainably high' 108% of revenue on player wages", *Independent*, 15 June 2023, https://inews.co.uk/sport/football/championship-revenue-player-wages-2411424

6 Jay Freeman, "Macclesfield Town FC wound up in High Court over debts exceeding £500,000", *BBC Sport*, 16 September 2020.

7 "Premier League clubs", *Deloitte*, https://www2.deloitte.com/uk/en/pages/sports-business-group/articles/annual-review-of-football-finance-premier-league-clubs.html

8 "League Attendance", *History of English Football*, https://www.european-football-statistics.co.uk/attn/nav/attnengleague.htm

Commercialisation

1 Louise Story, "Anywhere the Eye Can See, It's Likely to See an Ad", *New York Times*, 15 Jan 2007.

2   Emilia Kirk, "The Attention Economy: Standing Out Among the Noise", *Forbes*, 23 March 2017.

Privatisation

1   "Bundesliga price check 2023–24: The cost of German football", *DW*, 18 August 2023, https://www.dw.com/en/bundesliga-price-check-2023-24-the-cost-of-german-football/a-66547548

PART 2
A New Ideology

1   Ian King, "Fan-led review must not be diluted for apex predators", *Football365*, 25 November 2021.
2   Slavoj Zizek (2009) *First As Tragedy, Then As Farce* (London: Verso). p. 16.

Collective Ownership of English Football

1   Keir Milburn and Bertie Russell, "Public-Common Partnerships: Building New Circuits of Collective Ownership", *Common Wealth*, 27 June 2019.
2   "Liz Truss set to announce £130bn energy bill bailout", *The Guardian*, 8 September 2022, https://www.theguardian.com/business/2022/sep/07/liz-truss-set-to-announce-130bn-energy-bill-bailout
3   "Guide on Article 1 of Protocol No. 1 to the European Convention on Human Rights: Protection of Property", https://www.echr.coe.int/documents/d/echr/Guide_Art_1_Protocol_1_ENG
4   Ibid.
5   Keir Milburn and Bertie Russell (2021) "Public-Common Partnerships, Autogestion, and the Right to the City", in *Capitalism and the Commons: Just Commons in the Era of Multiple Crises* (London: Routledge).
6   Richard Fay, "Manchester United named as world's most popu-

lar football club", *Manchester Evening News*, 17 August 2019.

A Theoretical Funding Model

1 Mark Sweney "Premier League brings record number of sign-ups to Amazon Prime", *The Guardian*, 6 December 2019, https://www.theguardian.com/technology/2019/dec/06/premier-league-brings-record-number-of-sign-ups-to-amazon-prime

2 Graham Hiscott, "Secretive billionaire boss of Bet365 made £742,000 a day despite gambling firm's £72m loss", *The Mirror*, 8 January 2024, https://www.mirror.co.uk/money/secretive-billionaire-boss-bet365-made-31835855

3 S. Lock, "Gambling industry in the United Kingdom (UK): Statistics & Facts", *Statista*, 2020.

4 Daniel Geey (2019) *Done Deal: An Insider's Guide to Football Contracts, Multi-Million Pound Transfers and Premier League Big Business* (London: Bloomsbury).

5 Bill Wilson, "Manchester United and Adidas in £750m deal over 10 years", *BBC News*, 14 July 2014.

6 Callum Adams, "England's £160 World Cup kit is made in Bangladesh by workers on 21p an hour", *The Telegraph*, 31 May 2018.

Controlling the Market

1 Duncan Alexander, "Myth-busting the 2022-23 Premier League storylines – what is true and what isn't?", *The Athletic*, 24 May 2023, https://www.nytimes.com/athletic/4540648/2023/05/24/premier-league-storylines-mythbusting/?access_token=4872141

2 "Premier League: Clubs pay £263m to agents in 2019–20", *BBC Sport*, 24 June 2020.

3 Jason Belzer, "The World's Most Powerful Sports Agents 2019:

Soccer's Jonathan Barnett Takes Over At No. 1", *Forbes*, 21 October 2019.

4   Kieran Maguire, *The Price of Football: Understanding Football Club Finance* (London: Agenda), p. 73.

Creating a New Public Service

1   Sebastian Friedrich, "Salaries and salary ratio of the top 5 leagues in Europe 2020/21", *Football Finance*.

2   As aforementioned, the implementation of a salary cap needs to be carefully planned — there are a wide range of economic, political, cultural, sporting and social factors to consider. Moreover, in an unpredictable and volatile financial landscape, any suggested figures can become quickly outdated. Therefore, the following figures do not in any way represent a finalised model. Instead, the intention here is to propose a framework which can be modified and improved upon by knowledgeable experts.

3   "Deloitte's Annual Review of Football Finance: European football market revenues rise by 7% to €29.5 billion in 2021/22 season", *Deloitte*, 15 June 2023.

Levelling Up

1   Will Hutton (1996) *The State We're In* (London: Vintage). p. 223.

2   Keir Milburn (2019) *Generation Left* (London: Wiley), p. 118.

PART 3
Who Are We?

1   Plunkett, *End State*, p. 163.

2   Ibid.

3   David Winner (2006) *Those Feet: An Intimate History of English Football* (London: Bloomsbury)

4   Ibid., p. 263.

5   Luke McLaughlin, "'Disgraceful': pundit Graeme Souness criticised for 'man's game' comment", *The Guardian*, 15 August 2022.
6   Matt O'Connor-Simpson, "'I don't regret a word' - Souness refuses to take back 'man's game' comments after criticism from Lionesses", *Goal*, 15 August 2022.
7   "Football Fandom in 2021: Lifer? Statto? How UK football fan culture is changing", *Sky Sports*, 11 August 2021.

Consciousness Inflation

1   Mark Fisher (2009) *Capitalist Realism: Is There No Alternative?* (London: Zer0 Books), p. 3
2   Michael White, "Blair hails middle class revolution", *The Guardian*, 15 January 1999.
3   Mark Fisher (2018) "Acid Communism: Unfinished Introduction", *k-punk: The Collected and Unpublished Writings of Mark Fisher* (London: Repeater Books).
4   Milburn, *Generation Left*, p. 43.
5   Mark Fisher, "Reflexive Impotence", *k-punk*, 11 April 2006, http://k-punk.abstractdynamics.org/archives/007656.html
6   Mariame Kaba & Kelly Hayes, "A Jailbreak of the Imagination: Seeing Prisons for What They Are and Demanding Transformation", *Truthout*, 3 May 2018.
7   Milburn, *Generation Left*, p. 44.
8   *Fan-Led Review of Football Governance: Securing the Game's Future*, 24 November 2021, https://www.gov.uk/government/publications/fan-led-review-of-football-governance-securing-the-games-future/fan-led-review-of-football-governance-securing-the-games-future
9   Niall Couper, "Letter: Review of English football should be adopted in full", *Financial Times*, 26 November 2021.
10 Quoted in Milburn, *Generation Left*, p. 62.

11 "Press Release 21 December 2023 - A22 Proposes New Open European Competition", A22, 21 December 2023, https://a22s-ports.com/en/media/press-release-21-december-2023/

Building a Political Movement

1 Carl Shoben, "New poll: Public strongly backing public ownership of energy and key utilities", *Survation*, 15 August 2022, https://www.survation.com/new-poll-public-strongly-backing-public-ownership-of-energy-and-key-utilities/
2 Milburn, *Generation Left*, p. 58.
3 Corey Robin (2011) *The Reactionary Mind: Conservatism from Edmund Burke to Sarah Palin* (Oxford: Oxford University Press), p. 4.
4 *The Treaty on the Functioning of the European Union*, https://eur-lex.europa.eu/LexUriServ/LexUriServ.do?uri=CELEX-:12012E/TXT:en:PDF
5 Ibid.
6 FIFA Statutes, April 2016 edition, https://www.icsspe.org/system/files/FIFA%20Statutes.pdf
7 Botsman, *Who Can You Trust?*, p. 30.
8 Ibid., p. 62.

Conclusion

1 Leigh Curtis, "'Borrowed' - Nottingham Forest and Notts County fans in row over new Magpies attendance record", *Nottinghamshire Live*, 15 November 2021, https://www.nottinghampost.com/sport/football/football-news/nottingham-forest-notts-county-fans-6208389
2 David Graeber and David Wengrow (2021) *The Dawn of Everything* (London: Penguin), p. 68.
3 Gregory Bateson, "Culture Contact and Schismogenesis", *Man*, Vol. 35 (Dec., 1935), pp. 178-183.

REPEATER BOOKS

is dedicated to the creation of a new reality. The landscape of twenty-first-century arts and letters is faded and inert, riven by fashionable cynicism, egotistical self-reference and a nostalgia for the recent past. Repeater intends to add its voice to those movements that wish to enter history and assert control over its currents, gathering together scattered and isolated voices with those who have already called for an escape from Capitalist Realism. Our desire is to publish in every sphere and genre, combining vigorous dissent and a pragmatic willingness to succeed where messianic abstraction and quiescent co-option have stalled: abstention is not an option: we are alive and we don't agree.